Civic Engagement: Making a Change Together

Ronnie L. Smith

Dedication

*To my loving, caring wife, Amber C. Lofton, for she
has been the love of my life and continues to inspire
me every day with her free spirit!*

Acknowledgments

I'm forever grateful to two teachers who gave me the hope and support I needed in my life.

Jim Miller - Calaveras High School

He never gave up on me and made me do better. In my four years at this school, there were many teachers who tried their best to encourage us in the classroom, but Jim stands out as someone special because not only did his encouragement make a difference academically, but it also helped build self-confidence that will last a lifetime!

Seth Tichenor – Clatsop Community College

I'm thankful to him for getting me into the public service sector. Without him, I would never have been able to work with such a wide range of people and learn about their needs as well as my own.

To all the others that helped, encouraged, and made recommendations for this endeavor, I offer you my sincerest gratitude.

Also, I want to thank our beautiful kids who light up our lives in so many ways.

Contents

Chapter 1:

Introduction to Civic Engagement

"A small group of thoughtful people could change the world. Indeed, it's the only thing that ever has."

- Margaret Mead

Civic engagement is a concept that can be explained in several different ways. It is getting locals involved in politics and community affairs and training leaders from the grassroots level. I am writing this book to enlighten you all about the history of civic engagement and why it is so essential for us to understand and participate in it. I am very excited that you have chosen to read the book and hopefully take the first step in being our next community leaders and future state and regional-level politicians, and perhaps the head of state. It is my hope to get everyone reading this to have a discussion on community issues and work toward common goals. These conversations can lead to more significant ideas, and we can then tackle things together. We can create a system of community welfare where we are the politicians as well as the commoners. The benefits of civic engagement are numerous, and I will cover several of them as we go along. A few of these benefits include working actively to improve things in the community, responding to those who don't have a voice, and giving them a platform to air their grievances. This way, the silent majority and minority are both heard. I am introducing some key ideas here that I want to go into detail much later on. A lot of these ideas will be fleshed out in later chapters. The idea is to cover all the important concepts regarding civic engagement to give a greater understanding to all readers.

By the People, for the People, and from the People

Civic engagement pertains to getting the community involved at the local government level so they can air their concerns and resolve issues. It's about working together for the greater good of the community. I am writing this book to primarily discuss civic engagement in politics. This is because I feel that the general public can play a much larger role in politics. After all, they know what problems exist at the ground level. Civic engagement would be considered a hallmark of "for the people, by the people, and from the people." Why is this important enough to write a book about it? The answer is quite simple. Since we are responsible for electing our representatives in the senate, house of representatives, city governments, state governments, and the federal governments, we have a right to participate in politics too, at least at the local and regional level. The public needs to understand and realize the importance of civic engagement as this government that governs us is formed by us, from us, so we have to safeguard it and act responsibly. Everyone young and old needs to understand the basic and advanced tenets of democracy as it is the foundation that this country was built on.

Power to the People

As you must have noticed, the common denominator here is 'people.' It's the common person and what they think about issues that matter to them at the grassroots level. Our political representatives need to know what the common person is bothered or disturbed about. This is something that is very important to me because I want to encourage more people to participate in local government. I want it to start from the local level and then move up the ranks to the regional, state, and federal level. This is very important for us to train these people in politics by understanding issues locally so they can handle things on a national level. We don't get taught these things in our schools, colleges, and universities. At the same time, people who live in the communities and neighborhoods are more connected to the issues in them to better resolve them. It's civic engagement and community service at the same time. Therefore, we will increase our awareness of issues that matter to us because we are the common person here. We have every right to question our community and civic leaders and explain the issues that matter to us. We can disagree with specific policies and laws and propose amendments, then resolve those issues. We work together with our politicians to solve problems and learn the ropes of being politicians too.

As we move ahead in this book, we will discuss different facets of civic engagement and its benefits. We will talk about other ways to communicate with your community leaders, discuss issues, and work on resolutions. We can talk about civic engagement programs starting in school from an early age to adulthood to build future community leaders. The more we understand the system, the better we can tackle community issues with our leaders. The leaders deserve and expect our cooperation so that unless we don't engage, we can't resolve problems or bring about improvements to the quality of life and living standards. By educating ourselves and others, we can decide to venture into state and federal politics because we have gotten our feet wet in community politics. Civic and community engagement is the need of the hour, and with different voices being heard on the coronavirus SOPs, lockdowns, and so on, we all need to be on the same page. There is no better time than now to engage in civic matters because so much is going on. This book shall discuss, educate, and enlighten us about civic engagement, including the real-life efforts when they turned out successful. Throughout the book, we will discuss different models of engagement, their benefits, and cons to educate readers in choosing the best model that works for their community and what they should recommend to their community leaders. We will look at the evolution of civic engagement from the past to how it is today and how we can improve the ways it's done and educate and create awareness of it. We have enough tools at our disposal to make a difference, whether it's in person or online.

Defining Civic Engagement

There are several types of civic engagement, and those can be political and non-political. It's highly imperative that we understand all these types, and we shall cover all of them in this book for a greater understanding. There is an official dictionary definition, and then there's one we have to look at the context of how things work in our nation today. A report from New York Times[1] had cited an excerpt from the Civic Responsibility and High Education, Oryx Press, 2000 that defines civic engagement in the best possible manner: |

> *"Working to make a difference in the civic life of*
> *our communities and developing the combination*
> *of knowledge, skills, values, and motivation to make*
> *that difference. It means promoting the quality of*
> *life in a community, through both political and non-*
> *political processes."*

Similarly, Youth Gov's[2] research tells us that civic engagement is about "working to make a difference in the

---

1   *The Definition of Civic Engagement - New York Times. (n.d.). The New York Times. Retrieved June 8, 2021, from https://archive.nytimes. com/www.nytimes.com/ref/college/collegespecial2/coll_aascu_defi.html*

2   *Brennan, B. (2021, May 12). Cities Are Seeking Community Engagement and Are Willing to Pay For It. Social Pinpoint - A Place to Engage Your Community. https://www.socialpinpoint.com/blog/ community-engagement-public-participation-civic-engagement-lets-define-these-terms/*

civic life of one's community and developing the combination of knowledge, skills, values, and motivation to make that difference. It means promoting the quality of life in a community through both political and non-political processes. Civic engagement includes paid and unpaid forms of political activism, environmentalism, and community and national service. Volunteering, national service, and service-learning are all forms of civic engagement."

Therefore, it is imperative that community residents actively participate in civic engagement, especially in a growing community. These same people can participate via voting and volunteering and then learn valuable knowledge and skills and become a voice to inculcate positive action for the overall betterment of the community. I am writing this book as a way to empower people and take ownership of issues that matter to them, both political and non-political. The same people can empower others, and we can have a community working for its own benefit where everyone assumes a leadership role.

I am very hopeful that this book will achieve its goals and encourage civic engagement in all communities in America and enhance it where it's already taking place. The time is now to stand up and raise our voices and ensure that they are heard. Whether through voting or peaceful activism, it's about bringing the right change and representing democracy at the grassroots. I am sure that many of us will take that plunge by following the great Mahatma Gandhi by being the change we wish to see in the world. I am ending this chapter with a thought-provoking quote by one of the most iconic community leaders of our time - the one and only Martin Luther King Jr., hoping it can inspire change and get you pumped up by the time you're done reading the book:

"The ultimate measure of a man is not where he stands in moments of comfort and convenience, but where he stands at times of challenge."

Chapter 2:
History of Civic Engagement

"A willow deeply scarred, somebody's broken heart

And a washed-out dream

They follow the pattern of the wind ya' see

Cause they got no place to be

That's why I'm starting with me

I'm starting with the man in the mirror

I'm asking him to change his ways

And no message could have been any clearer

If you want to make the world a better place

Take a look at yourself, and then make a change."

– Man in the Mirror- Michael Jackson

Whenever you set out to make a change in the world, you need to start with yourself. Mahatma Gandhi once said, "Be the change you wish to see in others." Remember, the change in our world begins from within. From there, it grows into society, communities, regions, states, and on a federal level. We live in a nation built on the principles of democracy. Throughout our nation's history, we have seen civic engagement take place. We've seen some of the most outstanding community leaders emerge from ourselves with luminaries such as Martin Luther King Jr., Malcolm X, and others. These men were ordinary people like all of us and decided to take a stand for causes they believed in and sparked revolutions.

The Law-abiding Citizen

"No man is above the law, and no man is below it: nor do we ask any man's permission when we ask him to obey it."

-Theodore Roosevelt

When we look back at the history of civic engagement in our country, we realize that it has been embedded in our very constitution. Every citizen is encouraged to participate in it. The first thing every citizen needs to understand is that no one can ever be above the law, whether it's a regular citizen or a head of state. Every citizen needs to understand and obey the law of the land because that's how civil order can be created and anarchy can be avoided. Every citizen has specific duties to understand and follow, and we are outlining them here so this is reinforced.

While they may sound very basic to some of our readers, these elemental duties are more important than they read on paper. These are important to ensure the survival of our democracy. These need to be ingrained in our youth from a very young age so they can implement them all their lives as they get into adulthood and beyond. I hope that this book can stand as a guide for everyone to look at how civic engagement works and reinforce the civic duties of every American citizen. They are known as "civic duties," and there are five of them. Before we proceed further, let's define civic duty. According to Study.com[3], it is defined as "an action required by law for a citizen to perform." It further states, "Examples of civic responsibility include voting in elections, signing up for the military, volunteering in the community, participating in government politics, and holding public office."

That being said, do you know the five primary civic duties that every American citizen is required to uphold? If you don't, you've come to the right place. The five civic duties are as follows:

- Obey and respect the law
- Paying the taxes
- Performing jury duty
- Registering with the selective service
- Voting

3   *Study.com | Take Online Courses. Earn College Credit. Research Schools, Degrees & Careers. (n.d.). Study.Com. Retrieved June 28, 2021, from https://study.com/academy/lesson/civic-duty-definition-examples.html*

We'll go into detail with each civic duty and responsibility, so it will allow us to understand the historical impact better.

Obeying and Respecting the Law

This is the very first and most important civic duty because being a law-abiding citizen is everyone's responsibility. In order for a society to function correctly, every citizen needs to obey the law of the land. These include state, federal, and local laws and adherence to these, including paying any penalties for not abiding, for example, following the traffic laws and getting a citation for not breaking either of them. This is a fundamental responsibility and duty, and it's crucial to follow the regulations and encourage others to do so.

Paying the Taxes

Every American citizen is liable to pay taxes, and it's these taxes that contribute to making your state, locality, region, and community better. These allow you access to public schools, Medicare, defense, roads, infrastructure, and other amenities that your taxes go towards. It enables you to have ownership of your state, locality, community, and country.

Jury Duty

As a US citizen, you will be asked to perform jury duty at one time or the other in your life. The local court will ask you to be present at a hearing to give your verdict on a case, and that could be anything from traffic to legal to criminal. You act as an independent and unbiased observer and would not take sides but go by what the law states. The selection is purely random, and you have no access to the facts of the case until you appear at the hearing.

Selective Service

Selective service is part of the executive branch of the government that looks after registering men to serve a military duty when called upon. It awards access to federal benefits, such as student loans, employment, job training, and naturalization. Men between 18 and 25 are liable to register, and if they don't, they could be subjected to $250,000, including a prison term too inclusive of the fine or exclusive of it.

Voting

The last civic responsibility for citizens is to have the opportunity to vote for community leaders, state representatives, and even the head of the state. Voting is a huge responsibility because every single vote counts when it comes to electing the next head of state, mayors, governors, and other community leaders. That's how to make a change in the country, so your vote goes a long way in ensuring that.

Democracy and Civic Engagement

Throughout history, we have seen how democracy has involved everyone from the grassroots, and everyone has taken part in it. Our country is a living and breathing example, and history speaks for itself. Since George Washington became the nation's first president, the people have elected political representatives among themselves. There has never been a time where the country has been under dictatorship or martial law. We have set the example for the nations of the world to follow. The history of civic engagement goes back to the time of the founding fathers of the nation who made sure that every eligible citizen is allowed to vote for their representatives, and that happened all the way up to 2020 when the most recent president, Joseph P. Biden, was elected into office beating Donald Trump who had served the nation for four years. Every four years, this tradition has proven that power is in the hands of the people. Incredibly, since President Bill Clinton took office back in 1993, every person elected into the White House has served for two terms until Donald J. Trump. President Trump wasn't the most popular president and had diluted America as he couldn't fill in the shoes of his predecessor, Barack Obama. President Obama was elected into office twice and was, for the most part, quite popular among the people and raised the status of America globally. In many ways, he was a great PR man, and his then vice-president Joe Biden is now the commander-in-chief of the United States. Whether he is able to stick around for another term, we won't know until the election year 2024. It remains to be seen if he will uphold the democratic values embedded in the nation's blood.

The fact that Bill Clinton, George W. Bush, and Barack Obama spent two terms leading the country shows that they did something right to gain the public trust. At the end of the day, it boils down to the voters. Trump did not satisfy the American people enough to win another term, and we saw that he didn't take losing so lightly, which is a discussion for another day, or perhaps another book. This is an example of how meaningful civic engagement is, and the more people participate in it and use their right to vote, the better they will be able to shape the future of our nation. More than a right, it's a privilege that we can't take for granted. There are countries in the world that do not have such a strong democratic system and are run by monarchies or dictators. Communism isn't completely wiped off the planet as the People's Republic of China still upholds that system. Not to put down any other country, democracy allows every individual to exercise immense power. The election of representatives is so ingrained in our society that it goes from the city and town levels to the federal government. When we talk about history, there is no better example than the system that we follow. Putting power in the people's hands is vital as elected representatives will be held accountable, and our history has proven that time and again that justice will prevail. If we look at our presidency, leaders such as Richard Nixon, Bill Clinton, and most recently, Donald Trump, faced impeachment trials. You don't satisfy the public at large and don't deliver on your promises, and the chances are that you won't get another term in the White House.

Here, I'd like to talk about President Obama because he proved that it doesn't matter what your skin color is or what race you belong to, you can become the head of the state. He came from a humble background and made history by becoming the first black president of the United States. He also became the first president of color to serve two terms.

There are examples of immigrants who became naturalized citizens and held public office roles, and one fine example is actor-turned-governor Arnold Schwarzenegger. He was a highly successful actor who came from Austria. Hollywood turned him into a superstar whose resume is quite impressive. From the Terminator franchise to True Lies, Eraser, Predator, Commando, and the Conan movies in the 1980s and 1990s, he excelled every role. He later became the governor of California between 2003 and 2011. He is also the most recent republican governor. This is proof enough that you can be from any part of the world, and if you earn the right to be a citizen of the United States, you can take different public roles if you wish to do so. The only exception is not being able to run for the White House, as that is a right reserved for those who were born in the United States and aren't naturalized citizens. You're still able to make a difference no matter what position you take. Being a governor of a state is a huge responsibility, and Arnold Schwarzenegger fulfilled it.

If we look across the pond, we can see a similar trend; the mayor of London in the United Kingdom is Sadiq Khan, whose roots are from Pakistan. He has taken up that responsibility since 2016, and this is perhaps one of the more remarkable examples of inclusiveness in the world today. We should always judge individuals on their character and not their race or skin color. Every citizen has an equal chance to take any leadership position in the government if they are qualified and able to do so. History is written every day, and the late great King of Pop Michael Jackson said it so well in his hit song titled History:

"Every day create your history

Every path you take, you're leaving your legacy

Every soldier dies in his glory

Every legend tells of conquest and liberty."

There is so much truth in the above statement because we are creating our history every day. Since independence in 1776, America has been a shining example of democracy, and it hasn't been an easy ride. We have made mistakes but overcame them as no country is built in a day. The saying, "Rome wasn't built in a day," holds true because we had to deal with our growing pains, too, as a nation. We have seen civil war, civil rights movements, abolishment of slavery, and so on, and became the land of opportunities. People from all over the world have emigrated here to live what is very much known as the American Dream. It is a nation of immigrants as our founding fathers had immigrant roots. In my humble opinion, there is no country in the world where a person can rise from the ashes and become someone important. It's the principles of liberty and justice that have helped us throughout history. Civic engagement is very much part of this road to progress. No civilization or country can prosper until you don't give power to the hands of the people. That power also ultimately comes with great responsibility. At the same time, with great responsibility comes great power, too, so you should yield both with utter and complete fairness.

With Great Power Comes Great Responsibility

It is very much our responsibility to elect the right people for public offices, but there's something even more significant than that. The public representatives have to show that they're responsible leaders and are adhering to the democratic principles of the nation, whether they're a mayor, governor, or even a president. In the Trump administration, we saw some very questionable executive orders passed, and then some were eventually vetoed by the Judiciary. These executive orders wreaked irresponsibility. Protecting the nation from foreign terrorist entry into the United States, Executive Order 13769 was passed in January 2017 and later vetoed by a federal court[4] but later reversed by the supreme court. It wasn't his most popular executive order, as critics stated it was targeted towards Muslim countries and called a "Muslim ban." It allowed certain nations with a Muslim majority to be disallowed entry into the United States, including permanent residents. This shows that one must never abuse his position of power but issue laws that comply with the constitution. Perhaps, it's for such irresponsible actions that allowed Biden to triumph over Trump in the 2020 elections. President Trump has been called many things by his critics, such as racists, misogynistic, and very insulting.

---

4   *Patel, N. (2017, January 29). Federal court halts Trump's immigration ban. The Verge. https://www.theverge. com/2017/1/28/14427086/federal-court-halts-trumps-immigration-ban*

We hope that President Biden undoes Trump's mistakes, and we did see that with him revoking his older executive orders. Three of Trump's executive orders have been revoked since Biden assumed office.[5] Joseph Biden also took charge during the current covid-19 pandemic situation and has been very actively tackling problems since the pandemic became a pandemic. This is an example of solid leadership and perhaps would allow him to win over the citizens of America for another term in the White House and emulate his former president, Obama.

The Civil Rights Movement

When we look back at American history, one of the most prominent examples of civic engagement is the civil rights movement. It's by far the most powerful and emphatic movement that ever took place in the United States and changed the course of history as we know it. It was to allow African-Americans/ blacks to have equal rights and laws as the white Americans. This was a movement to end racial prejudice, discrimination, and inequality once and for all. We saw the rise of some of the biggest names of civic and community leaders to ever take a stand for such a significant and essential cause. The names include the legendary Martin

5   Feiner, L. (2021, June 10). *Biden revokes and replaces Trump executive orders that banned TikTok. CNBC. https://www.cnbc.com/2021/06/09/biden-revokes-and-replaces-trump-executive-orders-that-banned-tiktok.html*

Luther King Jr., Malcolm X, Robert F. Kennedy, former president Lyndon Johnson, Rosa Parks, and more. Many lives were lost in this cause, but this was the one reason why the US preaches equality today. Had that not been the case, then there would still be racial segregation and discrimination.

According to History.com[6], "The civil rights movement was a struggle for social justice that took place mainly during the 1950s and 1960s for black Americans to gain equal rights under the law in the United States. The Civil War had officially abolished slavery, but it didn't end discrimination against black people — they continued to endure the devastating effects of racism, especially in the South. By the mid-20th century, black Americans had had more than enough prejudice and violence against them. They, along with many white Americans, mobilized and began an unprecedented fight for equality that spanned two decades."

As you can see from the above quote, the civil rights movement turned ordinary men and women into heroes because they took a stand for what's right, and that's how they turned the tide and created history. These brave men and women paid the price with their lives so we can have a better today. The Jim Crow laws were against civil liberties, and therefore, a change was needed. You can only make a

---

6   *History.com Editors. (2021, May 17). Civil Rights Movement. HISTORY. https://www.history.com/topics/black-history/civil-rights-movement*

change and desire it if you are willing to fight for it and gather support for your cause. According to History.com[7], "The Jim Crow laws were a collection of state and local statutes that legalized racial segregation. Named after a black minstrel show character, the laws—which existed for about 100 years from the post-Civil War era until 1968—were meant to marginalize African Americans by denying them the right to vote, hold jobs, get an education, or have other opportunities. Those who attempted to defy Jim Crow laws often faced arrest, fines, jail sentences, violence, and death."

The civil rights movements to contest these barbaric laws are incredible examples of ordinary citizens' bravery and determination. Let me give an example of a simple civic engagement caused by none other than Rosa Parks. She is well known for taking a massive stand against racial segregation by not leaving her seat on a bus for a white person. History.com reports, "On December 1, 1955, a 42-year-old woman named Rosa Parks found a seat on a Montgomery, Alabama bus after work. Segregation laws at the time stated black passengers must sit in designated seats at the back of the bus, and Parks had complied. When a white man got on the bus and couldn't find a seat in the white section at the front of the bus, the bus driver instructed Parks and three other black passengers to give up their seats. Parks refused and was arrested."

7   *History.com Editors. (2021b, March 26). Jim Crow Laws. HISTORY. https://www.history.com/topics/early-20th-century-us/jim-crow-laws*

Parks was arrested for taking a stand, and that sent shockwaves to the rest of the United States, and it was Martin Luther King Jr. who took action on this. Thanks to the widespread support she received, she became recognized reportedly as the "mother of the modern-day civil rights movement." As a result, the black community leaders, inspired by her protest, joined hands to found the Montgomery Improvement Association (MIA). This movement was led by none other than the iconic Martin Luther King Jr. This role catapulted the baptist minister into the mainstream of the fight for civil rights for men and women of color in America. He became their voice and the architect of the movement in the 1950s and 1960s. What happened next was nothing short of sensational: the MIA then staged a boycott of the Montgomery bus system, which lasted a good 381 days. If you convert it into years, that's easily a year and two weeks approximately. This boycott promoted the supreme court to make unprecedented legislation stating that segregated seating was against the constitution on November 14, 1956.

Parks' courage incited the MIA to stage a boycott of the Montgomery bus system. The Montgomery Bus Boycott lasted 381 days. On November 14, 1956, the supreme court ruled segregated seating was unconstitutional. This is one incredible example of civic engagement that truly made a difference. Martin Luther King Jr. then became the champion of the civil rights movements and was undoubtedly inspired by the great Mahatma Gandhi to further his cause because he used nonviolent means to campaign for civil rights. The Irish rock band in the 1980s released this superb song in honor of

MLK Jr titled "Pride (In the Name of Love)," and the lyrics indeed paint the picture of a man who was fighting for love and equality for all.

"One man come in the name of love

One man, he come and go

One man comes he to justify

One man to overthrow

In the name of love

What more in the name of love

In the name of love

What more in the name of love."

So much happened in the civil rights movement, but it was MLK Jr. who believed in the cause so much that it wasn't about just rights for black people but equality regardless of skin color. Everyone should be treated on the same level of respect because it's about humanity at the end of the day. The idea here is if you want to take a stand for something, you can move mountains if you back a reasonable cause that can achieve long-standing and widespread support.

One critical civil rights game-changing event took place on August 28, 1963. That was the March on Washington, DC, that involved several prominent civil rights leaders, including A. Philip Randolph, Bayard Rustin, and Martin Luther King, Jr. This has gone down in history as a landmark event in American history and what most people remember MLK Jr.

for. There were over 200,000 people hailing from all races that gathered together in Washington, DC, for a peaceful march. The idea was to force civil rights legislation and to ensure job equality for all citizens regardless of race or gender. The most memorable aspect of this march was the historic speech by MLK Jr., where he spoke about his dream repeatedly. A few lines from his speech[8] are as follows:

> "I have a dream that one day this nation will rise up and live out the true meaning of its creed: We hold these truths to be self-evident; that all men are created equal.
>
> I have a dream that one day on the red hills of Georgia, the sons of former slaves and the sons of former slave owners will be able to sit down together at the table of brotherhood.
>
> I have a dream that one day even the state of Mississippi, a state sweltering with the heat of injustice, sweltering with the heat of oppression, will be transformed into an oasis of freedom and justice.
>
> I have a dream that my four little children will one day live in a nation where they will not be judged by the color of their skin but by the content of their character."

---

8   History.com Editors. (2021a, March 16). 'I Have a Dream' Speech. HISTORY. https://www.history.com/topics/civil-rights-movement/i-have-a-dream-speech#section_7

This dream was the dream of every liberty-loving American citizen in the 1960s who felt that race and creed were no reasons to judge anyone as we all are born equal and held equal in the eyes of our God. This has since become the battle cry for freedom and equality. The speech had a more significant impact as then-president Lyndon B. Johnson signed the Civil Rights Act of 1964. This piece of legislation had been previously put into motion by former president John F Kennedy prior to his assassination. The law was put into effect on July 2, 1964. The best part of this legislature signing was the presence of MLK Jr. and other civil rights activists as witnesses. According to History.com, "The law guaranteed equal employment for all, limited the use of voter literacy tests, and allowed federal authorities to ensure public facilities were integrated."

MLK Jr. was assassinated on April 4, 1968, and his death and tributes poured out from everywhere, including President John F. Kennedy's brother Robert. The latter held him in high esteem for his efforts to ensure civil liberties for all regardless of race and color. Robert F. Kennedy was serving as senator of Indianapolis, Indiana. This chapter would be incomplete without his speech.[9] to the nation where

9   *Statement on Assassination of Martin Luther King, Jr., Indianapolis, Indiana, April 4, 1968, | JFK Library. (n.d.). John F. Kennedy Presidential Library and Museum. Retrieved June 28, 2021, from https://www.jfklibrary.org/learn/about-jfk/the-kennedy-family/robert-f-kennedy/robert-f-kennedy-speeches/statement-on-assassination-of-martin-luther-king-jr-indianapolis-indiana-april-4-1968*

he announced the passing of MLK Jr. He was quoted to have said:

> "I have bad news for you, for all of our fellow citizens, and people who love peace all over the world, and that is that Martin Luther King was shot and killed tonight.
>
> Martin Luther King dedicated his life to love and to justice for his fellow human beings, and he died because of that effort.
>
> On this difficult day, in this difficult time for the United States, it is perhaps well to ask what kind of a nation we are and what direction we want to move in. For those of you who are black--considering the evidence, there evidently is that there were white people who were responsible--you can be filled with bitterness, hatred, and a desire for revenge. We can move in that direction as a country, in great polarization--black people amongst black, white people amongst white, filled with hatred toward one another.
>
> Or we can make an effort, as Martin Luther King did, to understand and to comprehend, and to replace that violence, that stain of bloodshed that has spread across our land, with an effort to understand with compassion and love.
>
> For those of you who are black and are tempted to be filled with hatred and distrust at the injustice of such an act against all white people, I can only say that I feel in my own heart the same kind of feeling. I had

a member of my family killed, but he was killed by a white man. But we have to make an effort in the United States; we have to make an effort to understand, to go beyond these rather difficult times."

Finally, the last few lines of "Pride (In the Name of Love)" by U2 in honor of MLK Jr. will always serve as the lasting reminder of what this man stood for and will be remembered for till eternity.

"Early evening, April four
A shot rings out in the Memphis sky
Free at last, they took your life
They could not take your pride
In the name of love
In the name of love
In the name of love
In the name of love."

Making a Difference

"Our citizens - naturalized or native-born - must also seek to refresh and improve their knowledge of how our government operates under the Constitution and how they can participate in it. Only in this way can they assume the full responsibilities of citizenship and make our government more truly of, by, and for the people."

– President Lyndon B. Johnson

History is all about making a difference, and the point is to own your responsibility and make the right decisions. We have seen in our history how people like Abraham Lincoln, Franklin Roosevelt, JFK, MLK Jr., and others have set examples of strong civic leaders, and these are the people we should emulate. You should start from your community and aim to lead the country one day, and that's how you can make an impact as you rise up the ranks. We've seen examples from our history of how men and women, young and old, have taken a stand for what they believe in and engaged in civic matters. They knew their causes were worth fighting and campaigning for and were willing to lose their lives for them. While the civil rights movement was a great example of civic engagement, another example is equal rights for women regarding suffrage.

This chapter covered the history of civic engagement since the independence of the United States. We talked about the civil rights movement and how men like Martin Luther King Jr., Rosa Parks, and others fought for equal rights for all and stamped their names in history, leaving behind an everlasting legacy. We learned about the lessons that history has taught us and how we can move forward and create meaningful history every day.

Chapter 3:
Why Civic Engagement Matters Today?

"If there is no struggle, there is no progress. Those who profess to favor freedom, and yet depreciate agitation, are men who want crops without plowing up the ground. They want rain without thunder and lightning. They want the ocean without the awful roar of its many waters. This struggle may be a moral one, or it may be a physical one, or it may be both moral and physical, but it must be a struggle. Power concedes nothing without a demand. It never did, and it never will."

- Frederick Douglass, Selected Speeches and Writings

These days, civic engagement matters a lot due to the overall increase in public awareness of community issues. Due to the rise of social media, community members and the general public have become very vocal about their concerns. They need a platform to vent them to the community leaders; they want their voices to be heard. The *pandemic* of coronavirus and movements such as Black Lives Matter has taken civic engagement to a whole new level, thanks to the rise and impact of social media platforms. The *pandemic* has brought about a host of issues that the community leaders and the community need to tackle together. This is why civic engagement is so critical now than it has ever been.

Speaking of the impact of civic engagement today, we need to redefine it in terms of the 21st century and plan for the future. Youth.gov defines civic engagement as "working to make a difference in the civic life of one's community and developing the combination of knowledge, skills, values, and motivation to make that difference. It means promoting the quality of life in a community, through both political and non-political processes."[10]

When we analyze the above definition, we come across a few things: making a difference in the community, community development, promoting quality of life, and participating in political and non-political processes. In today's world, there is more reason to engage in civic matters than it was before. Furthermore, there are so many opportunities to participate in it because social media has provided a voice to the common person that it didn't have perhaps a decade or two ago.

---

10   *Civic Engagement | Youth.gov. (n.d.). Youth.Gov. Retrieved July 19, 2021, from https://youth.gov/youth-topics/civic-engagement-and-volunteering*

Voice of the Voiceless

Just like history showed us excellent examples of civic engagement from the civil rights movement to President Obama's election, we saw our citizens make a change for the better. One or two brave citizens took a stand and became the voice of the voiceless highlighting issues that matter through whichever means they could. There are numerous opportunities to take a stand on important issues. Social media platforms have provided a new outlet for anyone to be a voice for those afraid to speak for themselves. Racial discrimination was a significant issue in the 1960s and 1970s in the US. Though things have gotten better over the years, it's not entirely eradicated. If it did, we wouldn't need movements like Black Lives Matter. People of color form a powerful minority in America, and their rights need to be respected like anyone else. There is no reason to stand quiet and be helpless. If there is a just cause, there is enough reason to go out in the streets, start campaigns on social media, or write letters to senators to protest. No matter what form of protest you use, you must keep it safe and civil. Use the option(s) that works best and can make the authorities listen to your voice.

Rock Your Vote!

Taking part in politics is one of the top forms of civic engagement, and there's one thing every citizen of America has taken part in since independence. It's none other than voting for an individual to the White House for four years and up to two consecutive terms. This political process is essential, and it matters today just as much as it did before. We have seen so many presidents over the years, and it has been a break from the norm. History has most certainly been made since George W. Bush finished his second term in January 2009.

There has been a significant paradigm shift in the last decade in American politics. We have seen a celebrity business tycoon take a seat in the White House for four years, a black president for two successive terms, and a female presidential candidate nearly triumphing in the race to the White House. This is an example of profound diversity which broke the norm that has been seen for several decades. Prior to Barack Obama, all presidents have been white, and neither has there been a female candidate going against a male candidate for the top spot in government. That female candidate was none other than the former first lady, Hillary Rodham Clinton, who later became the secretary of state under the Obama Administration. Later on, she contested the 2016 presidential elections against eventual president-elect Donald J. Trump. Interestingly, she had won the popular vote but lost out in the Electoral College count against Trump.

Hillary's attempt at winning a presidential election is proof that women can compete against their male counterparts and beat them at their own game if they try. No woman has yet won a presidential election, but that doesn't mean that it is impossible. If Mrs. Clinton could run for office, so could someone else, and we could see many women vying for that spot in the years to come. She kickstarted a trend, and it would be a historic day when we get to see the first female president of America. In terms of firsts, Mrs. Clinton was also the first democrat to run for office, while there has not been any female presidential candidate from the republican party as yet.

Ironically, this has already happened in the rest of the world. In Pakistan, Benazir Bhutto was voted into office as the country's prime minister twice. She first won the country's general elections as the head of her late father's Pakistan People's Party in 1988 and became prime minister; in 1990, she was ousted from office by then-president Ghulam Ishaq Khan. She won the general elections of the nation once again in 1993 and stayed in office until her own installed president Farooq Ahmad Khan Leghari ended her term prematurely in 1996. She is the only woman to serve as head of state of Pakistan.

Bangladesh has seen two women taking the office of prime minister: Sheikh Hasina Wajid and Khaleda Zia. Sheikh Hasina's father, Sheikh Mujib-Ur-Rehman, was both the first president and later prime minister of the newly-created Bangladesh in 1971.

Tansu Ciller was the first and only female prime minister of Turkey; she held the office from 1993 to 1996. In India, Indira Gandhi, daughter of Jawaharlal Nehru, held office twice (1966-1977 and 1980-1984). Her second term ended with her assassination. She is the only woman to serve as head of state of India.

History has shown us that women can also become leaders of countries, great activists, business owners, and CEOs. This goes to show how much progress women have made in the last 100 years or so. When we try to understand why civic engagement is so meaningful today, it's because of all the above factors.

The diversity in American public office extends to Hollywood and pop culture, too, when it comes to taking positions in government. Wrestling icons Jessie "The Body" Venture became the governor of Minnesota between 1999 and 2003. Most recently, Glenn Jacobs, better known in the WWE as Kane and previously Isaac Yankem DDS and Fake Diesel, became the Mayor of Knox County, Tennessee. Glenn Jacobs took office in September while still being reportedly signed to the WWE as a performer. Perhaps the most famous example of a Hollywood star taking public office in recent years has been the action superstar, Arnold Schwarzenegger, who became the governor of California between 2003 and 2011.

A Hollywood star has even taken a seat in the White House. Ronald Reagan was a successful actor before becoming the focal figure in American politics in the 1980s. He had two successive terms as US president between 1981 and 1989. This proves that no matter which walks of life you belong to or what your professional career has been, you could become the nation's president if you choose to be. Our history is undoubtedly full of examples who have made a difference at the highest seat in American politics, and there will be more in the future.

As necessary, it is to run for public office. It is equally important to participate in the voting process. The reason for such diversity in public office is that we, as the American public, have voted for them and have given them the chance to create history. That is an example of civic engagement of the highest order. Every vote counts, so we should always use our votes carefully. That being said, every person has a right to elect the best candidate in office as per their opinion. You could support the democrats, the republicans, independent candidates, or the Green Party led by Ralph Nader. You choose on the basis of your values and principles, so the person elected into office reflects those. This is why you should always rock your vote because each vote ends up making a difference and sets the future of our nation. Love or hate Donald Trump, he did become the president and survived four years in office despite impeachment trials and whatnot. He didn't get to win a second term, but he proved that someone with minimal political experience could take the highest public office in the nation. Any person can be the commander-in-chief as long as they are able to rally enough support and have a just cause that attracts citizens toward them.

Social Welfare

When a medium gives you so much exposure and access to people in billions, you have the opportunity to make a difference. You have a voice, and you can gather other voices to echo your cause. Several websites, such as change.org, facilitate causes and campaigns that matter to people. The more signatures people give to a cause, the more support it gets and allows a collective voice to get to the powers that be. While you're not out on the streets and holding placards, you're gaining support for a cause online. Social media is a much faster way to get your word across to a massive amount of people than it would be to do it physically or use traditional media outlets. You just need to get your word out and make it viral.

The most powerful platforms for social media are Facebook and Twitter because you can reach out to several influential people. At the same time, you could grow into an influencer and make an impact through your following. Another way to get your word across is through your personal YouTube channel.

Facebook

Facebook has clearly become the granddaddy of social media platforms. It has experienced explosive growth since its inception in 2004. Mark Zuckerberg, a co-founder, still runs the show from the top, and it's quite ironic that it was supposed to be a platform for college students to reach out to each other. It was like a virtual slam book of sorts, and it worked. Eventually, the platform was made to include others, and inclusivity contributed to its phenomenal growth. There are reportedly 2.85 billion active users that you can reach out to. You may not get a response from all of them, but even if a decent number responds, that would be splendid. Facebook has a variety of groups and pages where you can find like-minded people and raise awareness for causes that really matter. The use of appropriate hashtags and keywords will obviously help, and you could boost posts for a greater reach at a reasonable cost. There are definitely ways to get your point across through Facebook, all with a few clicks.

If you want to write long-form posts, Facebook allows you to speak and share it with your network, and then your network can share with theirs until it gets viral. You're doing civic engagement in cyberspace because we live in a time where most people check their social networks several times a day. They are more informed through Facebook than the local news. If you use Facebook to your advantage, you can have a successful campaign.

Twitter

Twitter is a top-rated microblogging platform. It has a host of major celebrities, and one of the most active users at a time was former US president, Donald J. Trump. Twitter is a way to interact with these celebrities and influencers and a platform to campaign for your favorite causes. You have to be careful with what you post, as inappropriate posts can be censored. Interestingly, Donald Trump has been reportedly banned from major social media platforms, thanks to his actions outside social media. Storming the United States Capitol with his supporters wasn't the smartest idea to begin with; it was perhaps an excellent example of civic engagement gone wrong. Therefore, act wisely on and off social media because, in our world, it takes a second for such events to become news and go viral.

Having said that, you have to keep your posts to 280 characters, make unlimited posts, and tag different Twitter handles and hashtags to get more engagement on your posts. The posts are called tweets and can get shared to other handles, which is known as retweeting. If you are able to get an influencer or celebrity to retweet you, you will be able to get a significant amount of engagement. The idea is to get your message across to people. This may or may not work with everyone, but at least, it's a way to raise awareness on issues and get people to talk about them and hopefully make a difference that way.

YouTube

Our lives have changed drastically since the emergence of the internet and smartphones. We have a limited attention span; as a result, we don't want to read walls of text or long social media posts all the time. Visuals seem to get the message across faster, and there's no limit to the kind of content that can be put on YouTube. The way it works is you create a channel, start speaking your mind, and eventually create a following.

Once you have a sizeable following, you can choose to monetize your content as more views give you increased revenue. However, despite being a monetized video-sharing platform, it's an incredible way to raise awareness for causes. If you do monetize your videos, you can use the revenues to further your cause. YouTube content creators have amassed views in billions; if you're able to reach a massive audience, you too can create a huge difference. You can get support for your channel by having subscribers to your channels and even members who will pay you to support your videos so you can provide them exclusive content. Patreon is an excellent way to get support for your video content as well. It's a way for people to support you to help you deliver better content.

If you want to use this platform as a means for citizen journalism, you could certainly do so. You can voice your opinions, get support, and reach out to the people who matter to achieve your goal. It could be anything from keeping your residential community trash-free or smoke-free to improving the neighborhood park or voicing your opinion on certain political leaders during election season. Perhaps, if you want to contest elections for your community or local school or anything, you can use YouTube as a platform for that.

The Coronavirus and Misinformation

For over a year, we have been facing the wrath of the Covid-19. It has brought upon a wealth of misinformation and false news because social media has been rampant with all of it, and it's spreading like wildfire ever since the pandemic became the pandemic. How does civic engagement help filter out the false news and ensure that only the truth is being shared? Similar issues cropped up around the time when the vaccines came out, and we heard so many conspiracy theories related to 5G, magnets, Bill Gates, depopulation, and the new world order.

Conspiracy theorists such as David Icke and celebrities such as Woody Harrelson, Russel Brandt, and others were speaking against the vaccines and 5G, and that's how a lot of the conspiracy theories became viral. Misinformation spreads fear, and that causes anxiety and stress. This, therefore, pushed everyone from doctors, health organizations such as WHO and CDC, and mainstream media to health professionals and experts; they were all tasked to clear doubts on the vaccines and 5G, and other pieces of misinformation.

Social networks such as Facebook went on a campaign to censor content by their users that would fall within the limits of fake news and misinformation. Many websites gained popularity, such as Healthline, MedicalNewsToday, and others, for disputing and debunking the conspiracy theories. Even universities and med schools such as the Johns Hopkins University School of Medicine jumped in on the bandwagon. Every knowledgeable person took the opportunity to debunk conspiracy theories through YouTube channels, Facebook posts, Twitter tweets, and more. Comedian and host Trevor Noah of the Daily Show actively spoke on how conspiracy theories were unfounded and had no basis for being true. His videos became very popular in combatting a trail of fake news. In some parts of the world, 5G masts were being burned down due to the conspiracy theories that these frequencies are helping spread the coronavirus or work in conjunction with the vaccines that are implanting a microchip in your arms[11].

---

11   *KELVIN CHAN, BEATRICE DUPUY and ARIJETA LAJKA Associated Press. (2020, April 22). Conspiracy theorists burn 5G towers claiming link to virus. ABC News. https://abcnews.go.com/ Health/wireStory/conspiracy-theorists-burn-5g-towers-claiming-link-virus-70258811*

The point is to ensure that every citizen is playing their part to curb misinformation and eradicate the fear that it brings. We all have to play a role in that with our families and friends so that we can protect them from false news and misinformation.

Black Lives Matter

Along with the coronavirus, the most important thing that the world took notice of was the "Black Lives Matter" movement. Last year, one of the major headlines in the US was of George Floyd and how he became a victim of police brutality. That sparked a massive movement that became popular as "Black Lives Matter." The original Black Lives Matter movement goes back to 2013 when George Zimmerman was reportedly acquitted of murdering a black teen by the name of Trayvon Martin. This movement sparked protests all over the US on social media, news, and physical ones, and it was to raise awareness on police brutality and discrimination against people of color. Since then, it has become a hashtag for racial discrimination and violence, and regular citizens have taken action against that.

The Black Lives Matter movement has become a compelling movement in the 21st century and a significant example of civic engagement. Thanks to the power of social media, it has multiplied. At the end of the day, the point of civic engagement is to take a stand on issues that matter, and this is why it matters so much today.

Changing the World

We have discussed several reasons why civic engagement has become so popular in our current political climate, thanks to the rise of social media giving every citizen a voice and allowing them to be heard on a regional and global scale. Civic engagement today can change the world because the more voices that are listened to, the more actions can be taken.

We also found out how much civic engagement can be used to combat misinformation and conspiracy theories, and therefore we can educate and inform people of the truth. It is our responsibility, and it is my hope this trend continues. This is the need of the hour as movements like Black Lives Matter depend on civic engagement, and we have seen how profound such movements have become today. Racial prejudice and discrimination can only be wiped off if our citizens take a stand against it, and this is why we need campaigns like Black Lives Matter. At the end of the day, all lives matter, but we must speak for those who have been maligned. These individuals need our support, so we should always look to further these causes in the best way we can, whether it's social media or a public protest. There is absolutely no doubt that we as citizens will take up several causes in the future because it is our civic responsibility. We must uphold this with integrity, sincerity, and honesty in today's rapidly progressing world.

Furthermore, it is crucial for every citizen to participate in the voting process. It doesn't matter whose side you're on;

your vote will make an impact. At the same time, each of us has a right to run for public office. Politics is an open playing field where history has shown us that people from all walks of life and humble beginnings have become heads of state. From people of color to women and celebrities, our country and world have seen them compete for public office. Whether these individuals won or lost, they set an example for others to follow.

Rising against oppression is another form of civic engagement that has always been historically relevant. So many countries have gained independence since the Second World War, whether against British Colonial rule or dictatorships. Democracy has prevailed, allowing citizens of oppressed nations to make a difference and give their fellow citizens a chance for a brighter future. It is the lowest echelons that always matter, as they have been the ones oppressed the most. Whether it is a minority or other individuals, their combined voices have done the impossible. From among them, leaders have been created and turned things around and created history.

From Abraham Lincoln to Muhammad Ali Jinnah, Mahatma Gandhi, and Nelson Mandela, these brilliant leaders have stamped their names in history by serving their people in the best way possible. Gandhi and Jinnah won independence from British colonial rule for India and then-newly-created Pakistan. Nelson Mandela spent time in prison but rose against apartheid rule in South Africa and became one of the world's most outstanding leaders in the 1990s. Such brilliant individuals have proven that nothing is impossible. They made it their duty to participate in civic engagement, take up legitimate and right causes, and ultimately change the world.

> *"It is said that no one truly knows a nation until one has been inside its jails. A nation should not be judged by how it treats its highest citizens, but its lowest ones."*

- Nelson Mandela

Chapter 4:

How to Engage with Community Leaders

"What really matters from the point of view of social capital and civic engagement is not merely nominal membership, but active and involved membership."

- Robert D. Putnam

There are several different ways to engage with community leaders as groups or individuals today. We have many resources and strategies to leverage social media to bring about causes that matter to the community and how to raise awareness on activities that are being taken to address them. This will allow us to gather more community support to further the causes and provide an open forum for community leaders and members to discuss issues that matter and come up with solutions. Even in the pandemic era, there are ways to engage as groups and individuals to engage with community leaders in safe public spaces, and everyone gets a chance to be heard. Technology has allowed us to remain in constant contact with community leaders and representatives outside of formal open forums and speaking engagements.

In the previous chapter, we discussed the importance of being involved in civic engagement and various offline and online platforms to create causes and discuss matters concerning our communities or nation. In this chapter, we will flip the switch and see how we can engage with community leaders.

There is so much that needs attention, and we need to get it across to the right people. This is because we all have a voice, and we need to be heard. One example that comes to mind instantly is the platform change.org. It's an incredible platform to gather support for causes and have petitions signed by people globally. These people can amount to thousands or more depending on the popularity of the cause. According to their website, "460,524,959 people (are) taking action. Victories every day." This means that four million people globally are raising voice for different causes.

You can have various causes based on your interests and beliefs. By taking one look at the homepage, you see causes such as "Let Students Keep Their Hair" and "Stop Using Labels as an Excuse! Teach disabled children to read and write #TeachUsToo." You see how people can use this platform to raise voices and get the message across to people who can make a difference. This is one very amazing way to connect with people who can make a change.

However, there are few ground rules when it comes to using platforms such as change.org to launch campaigns. First and foremost, honesty is the best policy, and we should stick to the facts, not opinion, and especially not controversial theories.

Suppose there are no facts yet because the organization is still analyzing all the data. Therefore, it may be best to wait until the facts are presented to start a campaign. It's okay to fear the unknown, but we need to work together as a team, family, and community.

It's also okay to ask for the facts and questions about the data being used. As I said before, it's completely okay to demand the best for the community. However, we need to do the legwork to look at all the data and participate in the public meetings. It does no good to say no without all the facts in front of us; otherwise, we could be supporting causes that harm us instead of helping us. Agencies such as federal, state, local, or community associations would be doing you harm if they acted without the data and the final facts. At the end of the day, we still may not be 100% happy with the facts, but we have to make the right decisions. Always remember these few things: knowledge is power and with great power comes great responsibility. Similarly, with great responsibility comes great power, so we need to use both wisely and find the correct balance between them.

Connecting (With) People

While Change.org is a way to connect with people who can make a difference, social media platforms are also excellent platforms per se. You will see so many people use change.org on Facebook, Twitter, and so on to advertise their causes. However, a platform like Facebook can offer so much more than a place to advertise causes. In fact, there is so much you can do on Facebook than on any other social media platform. Facebook offers this exclusive feature to create groups, pages, and communities for causes, and through these, you can reach out to civic and community leaders. It's incredible how powerful the platform is that you can launch movements from the comfort of your home without the need to go out in the streets and protest. You are safe, and you can rally for a cause and just reach out to civic leaders who will hopefully listen and deliver.

For every cause, you can make a page or group such as "Black Lives Matter," "All Lives Matter," and others that can bring in over 100,000 or more members. These are causes that need to be heard. When civic leaders see the strength, they use these to push their reputation up. See, civic and community leaders also want to increase their popularity, and by engaging with these groups and pages, they can achieve that.

The official Black Lives Matter page on Facebook has 744,000 members liking it. That's close to a million already, and it's growing. Civic leaders can have access to these 744,000 people easily. By engaging with such a massive community, they can get enough popularity to get them on board if they run for public office or some other leadership position in the future.

In addition to social media, there are other ways to engage with community leaders that have been discussed below.

Community Service

The best thing about social media is that word of mouth travels fast, and things can get viral very quickly. You can do the same with YouTube channels, but you can also engage with leaders on the ground. See, you can form groups within communities in your area and neighborhood. These communities can then nominate leaders who can reach out to members of Congress and senators or even mayors. You can do a lot by having potluck dinners and community events where everyone can meet, do ice-breaking sessions, and plan strategies on which leaders to contact and how to get their causes worked on.

You can hold in-house events and meetings, and then every person gets to speak at a time, and there can be a Q/A session. It could be anything from a clean-up drive in the neighborhood or a Covid-19 vaccination drive. In physical meetings, SOPs would be required to ensure it doesn't become a super-spreader event. Obviously, Covid-19 is a considerable drive towards vaccination drives that can help protect everyone and someday return to normal lives. These are concerns impacting all of us, so we need to get together for these causes. Of course, the best way to do it would be online; if you can meet people physically and answer questions about vaccines and their efficacies, side effects, and other concerns, you can convince a lot of people to get vaccinated.

Similarly, you can have Zoom calls with public and community leaders where so many people could safely participate from the comfort of their homes. Zoom calls require memberships for sessions over 40 minutes, so you can also use alternatives, such as Google Meet, Facebook Rooms, Telegram, and Microsoft Teams. We will touch upon these platforms below and see how they can benefit you individually and community-wise.

Google Meet

The best part about Google Meet is that you don't need any software but just a Gmail account to access it as it is integrated into Gmail. No matter what platform you use, you can access Google Meet because it works universally on all of them, whether mobile, tablets, desktop, or laptop PC. There are no time limits, and you can throw in community people and have a meeting wherever you are as long as you have a compatible device. A meeting can be co-hosted by 25 people. It's a Google product, and pretty much the whole world uses their services, so we can easily guess the users to be in billions.

It's very user-friendly because you don't need a separate membership. It works on a platform you regularly use, which is why you can get people connected easily and even get your community leaders onboard without hassle. You're connected in a few clicks. I would recommend this over other platforms, but the other ones do offer benefits too.

Facebook Rooms

Last year, Facebook launched a feature that allows people to connect via voice and video conferencing. Like Google Meet, it works within Facebook and Facebook

Messenger. It's one platform most people already use, and you're connected with four billion active users. So, you can have your groups and communities come together in rooms and have discussions and interact with community leaders. It's an incredible opportunity to interact with people who matter and can make a change. They will want to interact with a large audience, too, so that's an amazing benefit for everyone. It's a win-win situation, and everyone is happy. You can connect with leaders, and they can build their credibility and vote bank.

Telegram

While not as popular as Google Meet or Facebook Rooms, or even Zoom, Telegram is a messaging app to have 1000 people connected in a group with real-time messaging happening. It's like a chatroom with people connected on a common goal and issue. Also, you can throw in video and voice conferencing on a single call and have up to 1000 people on it.

If community leaders want to have direct conversations with people up to 1000 people in one go, they can do it on Telegram. It's similar to Facebook live videos where users can interact with the speaker via chat, but Telegram lets them do it with voice and video.

Telegram is getting popular globally and ranks alongside Signal and WhatsApp as popular messaging apps. Facebook-owned WhatsApp only allows up to eight people, as of writing, which is a far cry from 1000 that Telegram offers.

Microsoft Teams

Microsoft Teams is similar to Zoom and Meet, but it is more for inter-office communications. However, it can be used as a means to interact with civic and community leaders. You can build teams and interact with them and invite leaders to be part of those teams. The group size in calls is from 250 to 10,000 team members. This is a huge number compared to other apps.

Teams is useful, but you'll find yourself more satisfied with other apps such as Telegram, Facebook, and Meet because you don't need to install separate applications. The exception is Telegram, but it's a self-serving app for those not wanting the hassle of installing Teams and understanding how it works. It's more like Slack and not best for video and voice conferencing like the others.

The New Normal

Now that we have covered electronic and mobile platforms in great detail, we understand how this works in our new normal. When we speak of today, these apps are lifesavers because not everyone is ready to interact with others due to the Covid-19 pandemic and not reaching herd immunity as yet.

If more people get vaccinated, our old normal may return, but it's hard to say when that happens. However, we did witness the groundbreaking 2020 presidential elections in the pandemic era, and people did get out of their homes to vote. Donald Trump was knocked out of the White House by the current president Joseph P. Biden. Over 74 million still voted for Trump, so you can see how many had come out to vote because they wanted to make a change. Both candidates were actively campaigning in public and televised events. The civic engagement did happen, and we did reach out to our leaders through these media.

The new normal exists for everyone, and that's why it's imperative that we take a stand for our lives more than ever. We need to reach out to our leaders through online and mobile platforms and public events as per SOPs, so we can be heard. These leaders want to reach out to us, too, so we need to give them these platforms so the right change can be made. You can't make a change if you're not willing enough to do it.

In the 21st century, we have resources at our disposal, so we must take advantage of them. We have discussed ways to interact with leaders via web platforms and publicly, and we should continue this because change needs to be constant.

The pandemic can only end if we raise our voices together, reach out to the people who matter, and come up with solutions to benefit everyone. It's high time we use our resources and fight the pandemic together with our leaders. As President Obama once said, "Yes, we can," and we will!

I want to end this chapter with a quote from one of the best people persons I have ever seen on TV. This lady is a civic leader like no other and has brought so many key issues to the table through her TV show for decades. Even though she is no longer on air, she set the standards of how a celebrity host can empower a studio audience and a global audience at the same time and address matters that impact everyone. She is a true hero, and through her TV show, she allowed all of us to engage with her and vice versa. I am honored to share the following quote from her to close this chapter out.

"I think education is power. I think that being able to communicate with people is power. One of my main goals on the planet is to encourage people to empower themselves."

- Oprah Winfrey

Chapter 5:
Common Community Issues

"Alone, we can do so little; together, we can do so much."

- Helen Keller, U.S. author, educator, and disability rights advocate

There are several common community issues that need to be highlighted to our community leaders. These issues could be of the past, present, and future, as long as they impact the greater welfare of the community. They could be anything from building a new housing complex to schools, hospitals, or nursing homes. It could be discussing homelessness and initiating shelters to provide homeless people. It could be SOPs to move around during the current coronavirus crisis and pretty much anything the community would have concerns about. If we don't bring these to the attention of our civic and community leaders, we can't make progress as a society. As a community, it's our responsibility to ensure the welfare of all by involving our leaders in our issues so they can take the correct action and fix them. By staying silent on these issues, we aren't doing ourselves any favors. The pandemic has forced many of us to stay at home, and some of us are even without jobs. Thus, there are a number of reasons to engage the community and its leaders than ever before.

Every community has issues. The point is first to recognize them and see how you can use civic engagement to fix them. The idea is to get the community together to solve issues, whether it's online or in your neighborhood. In previous chapters, we looked at different ways to engage with leaders and how they engage with us. This time around, we will discuss concerns that matter. The most significant talking point on the agenda is the coronavirus disease; it is one thing that has changed our lives and has become a matter of public opinion, policy, and perhaps even legislature. This is because it concerns foreign and local policy. After all, the pandemic has impacted people globally. Therefore, public opinion matters where it comes to lockdowns and vaccines, for example. Our civic and community leaders have been at the forefront to bring the situation to our attention. However, we have to discern truth from fiction.

The Truth is Out There

The best thing we can do is to read news and identify whether it comes from credible sources or not. We need to verify sources and ask the people that matter, such as civic and community leaders, including medical bodies and health professionals.

The biggest issue plaguing us is the search for truth and dissipating fear. Fear is worse than covid-19 as it seeks to destroy our confidence and cripple us inside out. It causes stress, anxiety, and mental anguish, and hence, we suffer physically too. It is said that stress is one of the leading causes of heart disease. The best way to dissipate fear is not to listen to rumors and fake news spread on social media but get straight to the sources. This is where our civic and community leaders come in. The community needs to come together and tackle these issues. It is only then we can come on common ground and come up with solutions. Truth is the answer to falsehood, and we as a community need to take a stand on issues that matter and stand for truth.

Survival of the Fittest

We're living in times of the pandemic, and we have seen loved ones die in front of our eyes, and that's taken a toll on our mental health. Despite vaccination drives, the pandemic is far from over. There can be a lot of reasons for this, as there are vaccine hesitancy and conspiracy theories on the rise. Some people are afraid to get vaccinated due to the fear of severe side effects and possible death. The fear factor plays a huge role, and we have to help each other to ensure our survival.

The pandemic is truly the survival of the fittest. We've been locked in our homes for the better part of one year, and this has caused us a lot of stress. So many of us have lost our livelihood, and chances to earn a living are hard to come by. That itself is going to cause more stress and kill us faster than a pandemic can. We're living in what is known as the new normal. This is the time when we have to change our ways and work from home or be innovative; being innovative means coming up with clever ideas to start your own business online via social media and reach more consumers digitally than ever before. This is why the saying works each time: innovation is the mother of necessity, and with every chaos comes opportunity. Another saying fits here best: when life gives you lemons, make lemonade. The point I am making here is that even when times are tough, we need to get tough too. As it's said, when the going gets tough, the tough get going. When faced with challenges, we need not be afraid but brave in the face of the storm. By coming up with something unique, we can find an income stream or just look for freelance opportunities.

Freelance opportunities are more than a million online, and you can find them in several Facebook groups and pages. If you look in the right places, you can find simple earning opportunities such as data entry, personal assistant, content writing, and other things there. Freelancer and Upwork are two online platforms that provide similar opportunities. You can even advertise your talents and skills on Fiverr because that's the best way to find work in your community and globally. The internet is your best friend, and it's no secret that online shopping boomed in the pandemic as most of us were forced to order our necessities from home and not visit grocery stores or supermarkets, which also goes for other retail outlets.

Hold an Old Friend's Hand Virtually

In times of the pandemic, we need to work together and help each other out, whether it's financial getting groceries or other social issues. Obviously, many of us are under stress, and we need moral and emotional support. We can be guides and counselors to each other or refer our friends to proper therapy.

As I have explained previously, civic engagement isn't just about taking charge. It's also about holding an old friend's hand. Our community is like our larger family, so we need to identify our pain points and work on them. Family needs to stick together, and this is where doing this in the pandemic is so essential. There are people in our community who can't afford the luxuries that some of us live with. Those include jobs, access to basic necessities, food, shelter, the internet, and other things. Community welfare is the need of the hour, so we should reach out to our friends and family and see how we can get assistance for them. We, as a community, need to figure out the best standard operating procedures (SOPs) for us so we can avoid spreading the virus while still helping each other out. If we continue to help each other, then we can survive the pandemic. All we need to do is take charge and hold an old friend's hand!

Knowledge is Power

As we discussed earlier, fear has caused many to trust controversial theories rather than the CDC and WHO regarding protection from vaccines. President Joseph Biden has reportedly stressed vaccinations so that the nation could ultimately return to everyday life. To combat vaccine hesitancy, we must eradicate fear by educating the masses on their efficacies and benefits. We should highlight positive outcomes in the media rather than selling controversial stories and "bad news" to get higher viewership on television, clicks, and social media engagement. It's not helping anyone but the fear mongers whose only motive is to spread fear and cause anarchy and chaos. These are the reasons media outlets want to highlight when they should be working on promoting vaccines efficacy.

Forced vaccinations won't help, but educating the masses will encourage them to make the right decisions for their lives and loved ones. Knowledge is very powerful, and the pen is clearly mightier than the sword. Doctors all over the nation can talk about vaccines not to sell them for their manufacturers but to ensure that people know they're effective in taking on COVID-19 to keep us protected. It's these same doctors that should speak out against controversial theories and use all the platforms available to reach out to the masses.

Community Building

We've talked about community welfare earlier, so it only makes sense to bring up issues on which the community can come together. A few very common things in community building are perhaps the development of parks, playgrounds, schools, and even homeless shelters. There could be drives to clean streets and neighborhoods. The community can pool resources to make different community centers and places of worship because we do live in diverse communities. Other infrastructure developments such as improved roads, freeways, and the construction of hospitals are vital causes. Hospitals are critical considering the rise in emergency cases due to COVID-19. Our communities require resources, so we should ask our local leaders to get these made for us.

As our lives return to normal once again, we would need our parks, schools, and community centers filled with people again. At the end of the day, we're responsible for our communities and reaching out to the people who can most certainly make a difference. Parks are places where you can hang out with your family; children can let loose and we can all spend quality time with their loved ones. Schools are necessary so that our children don't need to go far to learn. Otherwise, they would need to be homeschooled, as some did during the pandemic. Then, some would argue that shopping complexes and malls will increase business activity and create employment in the area. Considering the resumption of ordinary life, many unemployed people could become resources at these places because human capital would be required there.

Another facility our community could benefit from will be gyms if we don't have any in our area. Keeping an active and healthy lifestyle is essential to our lives and gyms help build that. It is also one way people in the community get together as they can interact while working out, and some of them could even become gym buddies. The more opportunities we get to interact with each other, the better it is for our community's overall welfare. Gyms, once again, create employment as fitness enthusiasts can become coaches and trainers at these facilities.

Speaking of employment, that's a concern of every community because more people in the workforce would lead to reduced crime and poverty. These issues have become very important in the pandemic because people want to find employment again after being laid off. We should not always think for ourselves but for others, and that's the point of having a robust community. The idea is to work together for a cause that is greater than ourselves so that we can enjoy sustainable lives. We all have to come together and rise from the ashes, as the pandemic has put quite a few of us in distress.

Come Together!

The crux of this chapter is to bring the community together on issues that matter. The pandemic has given rise to more problems than we ever faced. As discussed, we had to deal with fear arising from false reporting, fake news, and misinformation. Education can separate the fake from the truth. The truth is out there, and we must know who to trust. We should never trust non-credible sources or discredited health professionals. We should conduct our investigations and due diligence and not believe everything shared over social media.

We have to work on community welfare and community building as that's how we can come together to take on various issues facing us, from unemployment, poverty, lawlessness, and crime. There is no better time than now to bring these issues to the open and connect with our community leaders to make a change. First, we need to be united on causes that matter so our leaders listen to us. One of us may need to take charge of matters because we need to come out of this pandemic very strong. It's in our hands, and we can either make it or break it. The pandemic has been pretty taxing for everyone, so we need a break from it. Since vaccinations have proven helpful in returning to normalcy, we need to educate our community leaders and people so that there is access to these vaccines. Vaccination drives in our community will accelerate the process. We can all come together to stop the spread of misinformation and debunked conspiracy theories on the internet and within our communities regarding vaccines. If we want our old normal to be our new normal again, it's time to act now!

Always remember that it's about all for one and one for all, and that's what being in a community is all about. I would like to end this chapter with a quote of a man who has inspired millions of Americans by teaching us "Yes We Can," and I truly believe that together we can all make a difference for ourselves, our families, and others around us! He came from humble beginnings and worked his way toward civic leadership, and became the first man of color to become the president of the United States of America by uniting our country together on several core issues to his heart because he had faced whatever we did growing up. He realized how important it is for all of us to come together and make a difference. He inspired us to become leaders just the same way he became one himself. Therefore, we need to be inspired by him and other brilliant leaders in our country's rich history and set examples the same way they did.

> *"The best way to not feel hopeless is to get up and do something. Don't wait for good things to happen to you. If you go out and make some good things happen, you will fill the world with hope; you will fill yourself with hope."*

- Barack Obama, 44ᵗʰ president of the United States

Chapter 6:
Actions and Accountability

*"In the face of impossible odds, people who love this
country can change it."*

- Barack Obama

Accountability is a significant area of civic engagement because it allows us to place checks and balances on our leaders. It is our responsibility to hold them to higher standards and ensure they deliver on their promises; otherwise, we can replace them with more capable leaders. Our public representatives are accountable to us, and we need to make sure they are following the policies set out within community engagements. If they have promised to take specific actions on any pressing issues, there has to be a way to hold them accountable. It could be anything from misuse of public funds, corruption, or not delivering according to their promises. Every leader is accountable to their representatives, and the community and public need to keep them in check at all times. The only way these leaders can continue to stay in their roles is to be accountable for their actions, acknowledge mistakes, and deliver on their promises. To keep things simple, we focused on the national and federal level and the presidency, but this is something to keep in mind at all levels of government, including state, regional, and local.

When you are a civic leader, whether it's the country's highest office or the regional or local administrative position, you will always be held accountable for your actions and decisions. This is because you were elected by a group of people or an entire population of a nation or state to work for their welfare. You weren't elected just for bragging rights and enjoy the perks of the public office leadership.

No one is immune to the corruption infecting our politics. Corruption can be seen at all levels, and no matter where you look, it's there in every country on Earth. The US has also not been spared from this pandemic - besides politicians being crooked as ever, some leaders make bad decisions without knowing what consequences will follow suit.

We have seen this with the likes of President Donald J. Trump and President George W. Bush. Both these elected leaders notably made some of the worst political decisions in the last two decades, which hurt our reputation globally. The biggest question here is that did we ever hold them accountable for their mistakes and disasters? They could have used an excellent PR firm to help them in their public appearances and decision-making. If America has suffered largely during these two decades, it's because of the horrible decisions made by two very terrible presidents that either won by luck or fluke, whatever you want to call it. In the last twenty years, 12 years were just hell for our country, and who can we blame? Should we blame ourselves for electing these leaders into office or the leaders for making some of the worst political decisions in our nation's history?

On the flip side, George W. Bush did serve two terms as president. While he wasn't the most effective president in recent memory, he must have done some good to warrant second-term reelection. We can't forget that in President Bush's first year, the US faced a deadly terrorist attack on 9/11 and lost over 3000 lives, including both of Americans and foreigners. The impact of that tragedy is still faced today, and Bush did lead us through those turbulent times. Although he may not have made the best decisions, he did lead from the front and gave Americans hope that they would not negotiate with terrorists and that the country would rebuild. It's not the easiest start to any presidency when faced with such a horrible tragedy just when you had gotten your feet wet in the White House. So, Bush does deserve credit for showing courage in times of terror and giving us hope when there was none.

Although Donald Trump was perhaps the least popular elected president and did not get re-elected, he did beat Hillary Clinton to the White House. Despite polls favoring Hillary Clinton due to her close association with the White House as a former first lady and secretary of state, she ended up winning only the popular vote but not the Electoral College. You can call it a cruel twist of fate, but Trump won and governed for four years. He was impeached twice but acquitted on both occasions. Love him or hate him, he had over 74 million voting for him in his reelection bid. Therefore, he was popular and did earn it. He still possesses a voice in politics and has several admirers.

That being said, accountability goes on both sides. We need to know better the people we elect into office because we give them the power to make these decisions that negatively impact our nation. In those 12 years covering two Presidencies, some of the worst foreign policy decisions were made.

Our history teaches us many things, and these are lessons that we must keep with us so we can learn from them. Making mistakes is a part of life, and sometimes we should be able to face them head-on without beating ourselves up. It all starts with identifying mistakes and problems and taking ownership of them. Then, we must learn how to fix the problem, and here's one mantra I'd like to emphasize because it fits so very well: fight the problem, not each other. If each of us focuses on the problem and looks beyond personal issues, any hurdle can be crossed, and the problem can be solved. If we adopt this approach in our lives, it will become very simple and save us from unnecessary difficulties. Our lives are way better off without complications, and this allows us to be courageous in the face of hardships, especially the current times we're living in.

I'm sure you understand that with any type of issue - no matter how small or big, they can become magnified by time which would only leave people feeling even worse off than before. If we stick to this, we will never raise a single voice to each other but work together to solve problems.

Problem-solving is a huge component of civic engagement. It's all about coming together to solve issues that impact all of us. It's about working for the greater good, and I wish more of our politicians thought on the same lines. Not all politicians are corrupt and insincere, but there are some who only care about their vote bank.

The Greater Good

> *"Democracy is not simply a license to indulge individual whims and proclivities. It is also holding oneself accountable to some reasonable degree for the conditions of peace and chaos that impact the lives of those who inhabit one's beloved extended community."*

- Aberjhani, Splendid Literarium: A Treasury of Stories, Aphorisms, Poems, and Essays

We must have a rule of thumb in which politicians must serve the greater good. They need to be held accountable for their actions. The greater good means best for the majority of the people because you can't satisfy everyone on an individual level. Still, on a group level, national level, or regional level, you can. Any place where your decisions impact a large group of people matters, and those decisions must serve good for those people. Now, when we're asked how we can hold civic leaders accountable for their actions if they're not doing the greater good for the greater amount of people, there are obvious ways to penalize them. For example, you can simply decide not to vote for them in the next elections and give a chance to those who you feel will bring about a change and be the voice for the masses. It's fine to give a leader the chance to finish an entire term and then assess their performance. A leader here could be a reference to anyone in authority, such as a city manager and a public service member. However, suppose an elected official does go over the line and make ridiculous decisions. They should be put through an impeachment process or a recall election, as it happened with Donald J. Trump on two separate occasions. We have to call a spade a spade, and there were a few crucial mistakes that earned President Bush criticism. George W. Bush has been held responsible by his critics for risking the lives of so many American soldiers in a preemptive strike on Iraq to find weapons of mass destruction where there were none. The consequences of these actions were a chain of events that caused chaos in Iraq. Political critics termed the entire pre-emptive strike as an invasion of Iraq that made the US look more akin to an imperialist power.

Unfortunately, political critics were able to use the Iraq campaign as an excuse to attack President Bush. The decision to strike Iraq was regarded as a result of horrible intelligence. Since America is a country that believes in freedom and civil liberties, truth, and justice, this strike made us more like a colonial power. Even though President Bush seemingly had peaceful intentions, we misrepresented ourselves because we have always called ourselves champions of democracy. We aren't supposed to be an autocratic dictatorship out to conquer other countries, and if that's the impression we're giving, it's not a good thing for our image at all. It's very important our leaders stick to the principles of the founding fathers. The greater good can also be for the world because we have a massive say in global politics, but we shouldn't abuse that power we have. As stated before, with great power comes great responsibility, and with great responsibility comes great power. We have a responsibility towards the world being perhaps the lone superpower, and our foreign policy decisions can make and break our image. We all know that when America sneezes, the world catches a cold. Anything that impacts us, therein impacts the world too. Therefore, it's imperative our leaders recognize this and act on it. By making the correct decisions, we will enhance our image and protect our principles at home and abroad.

The Four-Year Itch

"Democracy transformed from thin paper to thick action is the greatest form of government on Earth."

- Martin Luther King Jr.

When we look at accountability, we are judging how our leaders are performing according to their promises. Every four years, we elect a new president or keep a sitting first-term president in office for another term. Our votes have enormous power, and we can make a massive difference by electing the right leaders. No leader is perfect, and all our elected presidents came in and promised change. That being said, they did make mistakes as they're only human after all. Some presidents were more popular than the others, but they all deserved their time in the White House. We need to assess them on their strengths, weaknesses, and the decisions they made. We would have to follow the same practice with current President Joseph P. Biden. His followers are hoping that he continues the progress President Obama made when he was in office. Obama has been highly regarded as a progressive president, but there is no doubt he has made mistakes and has admitted them, such as the strike on Libya to remove Colonel Muammar Gaddafi from power. Therefore, he would be held accountable just as the others who were in charge before and would be after him.

The best way to hold out leaders accountable is to not give them a chance if they have not delivered on their promises. If they haven't, we need to elect a new leader and give that person a chance to prove themselves. That's how it works every four years, and we, the people, are responsible for this. If we make the right decisions in voting for the right people, they shall deliver, so it's our responsibility. Then again, we have to look out for the greater good, so our vote counts for that too.

There can be a formula to decide if the president delivers on promises or not. First, we must write down their campaign promises and then see if they have delivered on each of those promises every four years. That's an excellent way to hold them accountable, and if they don't work during their term, we can take action and protest because we have a voice, and we shouldn't be afraid to use it.

You're the Voice

As we close on this chapter, we must recognize how powerful our voice is. We have the power to take action, protest, and hold our leaders accountable. We can vote them into the office and take them out of office. By having a voice, we need to be accountable to elect the right leaders in office. Our vote is our voice, so use it right because our country's leadership depends on it. We shall hold our leaders to the higher standards of sound leadership and good governance and let them know that they're not delivering on their word. We should help them and guide them and make a change. That's how we can use our voice for the greater good!

"Ask not what your country can do for you; ask what you can do for your country."

- John F. Kennedy

Chapter 7:

From Citizens to Leaders

"That this nation, under God, shall have a new birth of freedom – and that government of the people, by the people, for the people, shall not perish from the Earth."

- Abraham Lincoln

When community members discuss issues with their leaders and bring about change, they are also trained to be leaders. Therefore, it is extremely important for all of us as community members to become leaders of our respective communities so we can later do similar community engagements. To be effective civic leaders, we must learn how we can contribute to community engagements and learn what it takes to be a leader and tackle various issues. It was a community member that is a leader now, and we all need to grow into one at some point.

Since democracy is about a government for the people, by the people, and of the people, it's the people that matter the most. People are mentioned thrice in the statement by

Abraham Lincoln, so when we talk about of, for, and by the people, it means that it's one of us who eventually takes charge and becomes a leader. We groom leaders amongst ourselves and take our communities, states, and nations forward. Every individual who has taken up a leadership role, whether community or the White House, was once a regular person like us. The point is that in a democracy and a free society like ours, a leader would rise amongst us to light our darkest hour, which has happened on so many occasions. I think that there have been two recent examples that come to mind. The first example was Barack Obama when he became president in January 2009. He took over from George W. Bush, who had just finished his second term on a horrible note. The country was in the midst of a terrible recession as major financial institutions were in crisis. At the same time, millions of dollars were spent on defense thanks to military campaigns in Iraq and Afghanistan. The American military was sent on a military campaign to Iraq based on the pretext of weapons of mass destruction, aka nuclear weapons stockpiles, thanks to shoddy intelligence and apparently a personal vendetta against Saddam Hussein. There was no doubt that Saddam Hussein was no saint either, but the approach to remove him from power backfired, and it could have been handled better.

President Obama inherited the government in shambles but fixed everything in his first few years and got the country back on track. Although divisive, his Affordable Care Act, aka Obamacare, was the first move towards federal health care. At least, Obama did the best he could to rescue the nation, and his eight years have been considered the best in the last two decades. The second example is President Joe Biden. Biden inherited the government from Donald J. Trump, and the less said about Trump, the better. Biden was Obama's vice president for eight years and will hopefully continue the good work that his former commander-in-chief did. We can assess his performance after four years, and then the American public can decide if he deserves another stay in the White House for a further four years.

The point is these were ordinary people and became presidents. President Trump was never actively involved in politics as he was mostly known as a construction magnate and a cutthroat businessman whose name is on major real estate and landmarks globally, such as the Trump Tower in New York City. He had also made appearances in movies such as Home Alone 2: Lost in New York and The Little Rascals, and hit television shows including The Fresh Prince of Bel-Air, Spin City, Sex and the City, and The Nanny. He also was a major presence on WWE television in his scripted feud against the billionaire owner Vincent Kennedy McMahon. He made appearances in WrestleMania 23, where the feud culminated in Trump winning the match as his chosen wrestler Bobby Lashley won against McMahon's chosen wrestler Umaga. The stipulation of the "Battle of the Billionaires" match was that the winning billionaire would shave the loser's head bald. Therefore, Donald Trump shaved Vince McMahon's head bald. He later became a reality star between 2008 and 2017 as the producer of "The Apprentice." He starred in the show and was famous for firing contestants who didn't meet his standards. As you can see, Trump didn't come from a political background and just gained celebrity status through his business deals and media appearances.

Similarly, Barack Obama came from humble beginnings. His mother was an American who married a Kenyan student. He was not born into a majorly rich family. His father, Barack Obama Senior, left him and his mother when he was just two years old. It is said that he passed away in an accident 19 years later. UVA Miller Center writes this about Obama:

> *"After his parents divorced, Obama's mother married another foreign student at the University of Hawaii, Lolo Soetoro of Indonesia. From age six through ten, Obama lived with his mother and stepfather in Indonesia, where he attended Catholic and Muslim schools. 'I was raised as an Indonesian child and a Hawaiian child and as a black child and as a white child,' Obama later recalled. 'And so, what I benefited from is a multiplicity of cultures that all fed me.'"[12]*

Obama studied at prestigious institutions such as Columbia University and Harvard Law School and became a lawyer. Through his law career, he eventually entered politics and the rest, as we know, is history. His triumph

12   *Consulting Editor: Michael Nelson. (2016, October 4). Barack Obama: Life Before the Presidency. Miller Center. https://millercenter. org/president/obama/life-before-the-presidency*

in the 2008 elections would always be regarded as historic and groundbreaking. His vice president and now-current president, Joseph P. Biden, also came from a regular family and wasn't born with a silver spoon. Here's what the UVA Miller Center says about President Biden's beginnings:

"Joseph Robinette Biden Jr. was born on November 20, 1942, in Scranton, Pennsylvania, as World War II raged overseas. The first child of Catherine Eugenia "Jean" Finnegan Biden and Joseph Robinette Biden Sr., Joey, as he was known, was a scrappy kid from a working-class Irish Catholic family. Biden's father prospered during the war when an uncle gave him a job in his lucrative manufacturing company that provided sealant for marine merchant ships. Joe Sr. left Scranton to run the Boston office; he lived the high life, driving fast cars, hunting, and haunting the polo fields. But after the war, his fortunes reversed, and Joe Sr. found himself adrift. After a couple of failed business ventures, he returned to the coal-mining town of Scranton, where he took what work he could get to support the family. By now, Joe Jr. had been joined by his sister Valerie; two brothers, James and Frank, would complete the family.[13]"

---

13   Levingston, S. (2021, January 19). Joe Biden: Life Before the Presidency. Miller Center. https://millercenter.org/joe-biden-life-presidency

Like Obama, Biden went through institutions like Syracuse University Law School, entered the law field, and eventually politics. He eventually became the vice president in the Obama administration and later the president last year after beating Trump to the White House. The idea behind these brief histories was that anyone could enter politics in the same way Obama and Biden did, and then there are some like President Trump who entered politics as a celebrity. Regardless of your background, you could enter politics and run for office.

History has proven time and again how regular folks like us have gone on to do such amazing things, and one of them is exemplary civic leadership. You can't be a leader if you're not a citizen, and you need to be a law-abiding one to take a leadership role. You need to set the right example for your followers so they can back you up. This book speaks on civic engagement, and we've discussed everything from reaching out to community leaders and using today's technology, but we're now talking about becoming leaders. It's all about doing the right thing, and I've been preaching this throughout this book.

The Model Citizen

"To be a good citizen, it's important to be able to put yourself in other people's shoes and see the big picture. If everything you see is rooted in your own identity, that becomes difficult or impossible."

- Eli Pariser

As stated previously, the only way to be a solid leader is to be a model citizen. You have to prove by your actions, not just words, for people to believe in you and support your leadership goals, whether it's to run for mayor or president. You need to build your leadership skills from the grassroots level by taking advantage of opportunities at the school and collegiate levels. For example, you can run for leadership positions in the student council, class president, or anything else when you're in school. You could be captain of the football team if you're an athlete. That's how it all begins. At the same time, practice solid and sound citizenship everywhere you go. Make sure you respect the law of the land and be good to others.

If you keep your streets and your neighborhood clean, help those in need, and initiate campaigns for the betterment of your community, you prove to be a model citizen. You educate your community about the good work the civic leaders are doing or hold them accountable for their actions; others will see leadership skills in you and back you up when it's time for you to run for office. You need to hold strong ideals and principles and be a person of your word. I can't stress enough how important it is for everyone to see that you genuinely care about the community's welfare. You can't fake it because people would see right through you. If you make any wrong moves, you'll be the next notorious celebrity on social media, and that's never going to help you win anyone over.

An article in The Guardian speaks very intricately of what it takes to be a model citizen. Excerpts are as follows:

"Model citizens forward mail to the previous occupants of their house for 17 years after they've moved. They do their income tax return on the afternoon of April 5 to catch the first post on the 6th. And they fill it in with black ink and clear capitals. They also declare income found down the back of the sofa.

"Model citizens don't drop rubbish. They actually pick it up and put it into bins. If there are no bins, they will take eight crushed beer cans home in their handbag. Model citizens volunteer for things. They are on the board of governors of the local school, even if they don't have children. They shake charity tins for 12 straight hours.

"Model citizens can't see a policeman without putting on the kettle. As members of Neighborhood Watch, they catalog every movement of everything so that crimes can be re-enacted in more detail than they were actually committed. Model citizens keep off the grass of all descriptions. The idea of them walking across a restricted municipal lawn is as unlikely as them lighting a seven-inch spliff in Waitrose.

"In municipal swimming baths, model citizens don't run, canoodle, bomb or leave plasters by the pool. They also have a shower before entering the baths. They swim in lanes even if there aren't any, and they keep a weather eye out for children suffering from negative buoyancy.

"When traveling by train, they have their ticket ready for inspection at all times. They also like to lightly eavesdrop in case they can be of assistance with timetable inquiries. On alighting from the train, the model citizen will have remembered, checked, and counted all his belongings and taken them with him. He will also close as many doors as needed to expedite the train's departure. Similarly, the airborne model citizen will keep his seat belt loosely fastened even when moving up and down the aisle."[14]

The above is written from a British perspective, but the idea is that a model citizen is a role model for others to follow, hence the word model attached to "citizen." If you want to create a following, you must make the right moves and do it very sincerely and genuinely; that goes without saying. It's the best way to win hearts, and that's how you can fulfill your civic leadership ambitions.

If you're in school, you must volunteer for any community service opportunity you can get, whether to clean the streets or neighborhoods or help underprivileged families and children. You have to show that you care about

---

14   *Browning, G. (2017, December 1). How to. . . be a model citizen. The Guardian. https://www.theguardian.com/lifeandstyle/2002/mar/30/ weekend.guybrowning*

the community you belong to and go above and beyond the call of duty to serve that community. You can participate in any goodwill activities that show you committing acts of kindness so you can get noticed. It could be giving food, care, and shelter to deserving families and people. Any action that can make a difference in society will be appreciated, and build your resume.

The Model Leader

"I think a role model is a mentor – someone you see
on a daily basis, and you learn from them."

- Denzel Washington

Many high schools and colleges have promoted conferences such as the National Model United Nations (NMUN) and the American Model United Nations. These Model United Nations conferences allow teams from different universities and high schools to be delegates of different countries and conduct real-world diplomacy with each other. It's all roleplaying but grounded in reality. You have to present speeches, conduct dialogues with allies, and vote on resolutions. Such conferences are excellent in inculcating leadership skills in young adults, especially those who are considering foreign service. The opportunity to play pretend ambassadors and speakers at a mock United Nations setup is incredible because you learn so many skills. The NMUN conference goes further ahead by having the opening and closing sessions inside the genuine UN General Assembly. If you want to learn some leadership skills and tackle real-world problems, this is one excellent way to go. If you're ambitious about running for president or becoming the secretary of state or even the national security advisor, the Model UN conferences can equip you with those skills.

When we talk about being a model leader, it's about never forgetting your roots. You should never forget where you came from when you get to the position of an essential civic leader such as a presidential candidate. It's always wise to stay humble and grounded as a leader, whether it's the White House or a corporation. Perhaps the finest example of such a leader in recent history is Nelson Mandela, and another would be Barack Obama.

Donald Trump has been criticized as a misogynist, racist, and crude by his opponents because of his public persona and how he has represented himself on social media. He may not be a model president but deserves recognition for leading the country for four years and still has quite a following. Exemplary leaders in national and global circuits past, present, and future, include luminaries as the aforementioned legendary Nelson Mandela, Mahatma Gandhi, Abraham Lincoln, Martin Luther King Jr., Malcolm X, Kofi Annan, John F. Kennedy, and Barack Obama. When you're a leader, you need to take initiatives on causes that matter, such as global peace, combatting COVID-19, peaceful relations with neighbors, rehabilitation of refugees, keeping control of law and order, eradication of poverty, promotion of education, and making it accessible to all. These are all excellent examples of positive leadership that would make you a model leader. Mimeo lists seven traits for an effective manager. Still, these would apply to civic engagement too: present a positive attitude, earn and build trust, exhibit integrity, lead and inspire, make time for employees, learn about your employees, and offer support and encouragement.[15]

A positive and winning attitude, trust-building, integrity, and being there for citizens are all ingredients required for being an effective civic leader. It's also about empowering people so you can groom future leaders. Once you take the initiative to do what's right, others will follow suit. At the end of the day, what matters most is serving the people who allowed you to become a leader in the first place. You do that, and you'll earn their trust, and you will be able to get another term in office. No leader is perfect, so it's always important to acknowledge mistakes. A sound leader is one who does not shy from admitting mistakes and making amends for them. It's highly imperative to follow self-accountability because others will if you don't.

We have so many examples of global political leaders that we mentioned here, and these should be our role models. We should learn about their lives and incorporate their traits in ourselves so we can execute effective leadership with humility and integrity. Be just, wise, and fair when it comes to dealing

---

15   *Leadership: 7 Ways to Become a Role Model Manager. (2021, March 22). Mimeo.Com. https://www.mimeo.com/blog/leadership-role-models/*

with those you serve. Empathy is an equally important trait to possess. If you understand the needs of the people well enough, you shall make the right decisions. Your followers and citizens look up to you, so you shouldn't let them down. Ask yourself what kind of a person you wanted your leaders to be and be that person. When Mahatma Gandhi said, "Be the change you wish to see in the world," he meant go out there and be that change, and make a difference in people.

You should show effective leadership in all walks of life as the head of a family, a corporation, as a teacher, or just a mentor. These are all ways to communicate excellent leadership and lead from the front. I feel that teaching is a wonderful way to express and acquire leadership skills because you are making a difference in the lives of students by teaching them life skills, academics, and being their mentors. If your students end up becoming inspirational leaders, they will always credit you as their source of inspiration. You should inspire and be inspired, and that literally is what it takes to be a great leader. If you want to be a model leader, then be a model citizen first and prove your worth to the people whose support you require. Once you establish your worth, you will earn their respect, admiration, love, and support the entire time you stay in public service and civic engagement. It starts from being a solid model citizen first and then developing into a role model civic leader. Our world and nation need such leaders now more than ever, so we should take the initiative.

Public Servants

"Be the flame of fate, that torch of truth to guide our
young people toward a better future for themselves
and for this country."

- Michelle Obama

Our democracy is built on the principle to put people first, as our founding fathers wanted. Our leaders have come from us and will continue to do so till the time this system is in place. We have to protect the values taught to us by our founding fathers and serve the people. We need to protect and care for our people as leaders, just like we do for our children. It's not really about getting the popular vote; it's about making a difference. The public wants change, and that too a positive change, so deliver it. By pursuing strong civic engagement activities, we raise ourselves to the level where we could be considered leaders. It needs to start from the grassroots, that is, the community level, and go all the way to presidency. If you win the position by vote, be an honorable public servant; then only can you make the necessary change. Admit mistakes and be accountable to the public. Stay humble always. This, in summary, is how we ought to serve the public. The world and our nation need positive role models so we could very well be the next one so let's take the initiative to build ourselves to that level because one person can make a difference. It starts from the power of one!

"I've always thought of myself as a role model even before being a celebrity. I've always been doing charity work and volunteering in the community since I was 8, so when you do that, I think you just assume that role when you put yourself out there."

- Eva Longoria

Chapter 8:
Educational Programs in Schools and Higher Education Institutions

"Civic engagement is very important. We all live here together, and we need to look out for one another."

- Elizabeth Goreham

Children should be made aware of civic engagement from a young age and be taught to write letters and emails to their community leaders. These kinds of programs will help them become responsible adults and be more active in participating in community events and engagements. Educational and awareness programs will help develop a new breed of community leaders trained since childhood on tackling community issues. There are several programs and initiatives that schools can undertake to teach our children civic engagement and community service.

Civic leadership and engagement should be made compulsory for children as they start school and are old enough to understand its dynamics. This is the best way to inculcate the knowledge of power and responsibility to them. These two traits are absolutely essential for children to learn until they reach young adulthood. It would be best to get children involved in civic and community activities at a very young age. They would get a strong feeling of community service this way. The idea is to let our children know it's essential to serve the public trust. They need to be taught how to be a noble and model citizen and contribute to society and community in the most effective ways. We need to give them the tools, the education, and access to ways on how to participate in civic engagement and offer rich learning opportunities.

Youth in Progress

"Every great dream begins with a dreamer. Always remember, you have within you the strength, the patience, and the passion to reach for the stars to change the world."

– Harriet Tubman

Our youth are our biggest asset, and we need to groom and mold them so they can differentiate between right and wrong and grow up respecting the law. The responsibility is in the hands of our teachers to teach children the correct values and responsibilities so that they can practice civic engagement from a very young age. It could be a drive to eradicate hunger, or a bake sale for charity, or something else. It's about joining hands with other community members to make a difference in people's lives.

According to Children International, "Youth civic engagement activities and programs are critical for empowering young people to develop their skills and talents; participate in political, economic and social conversations; and become agents of positive change in their communities."[16] It would very much help teach children the basics of the constitution and American history, so they learn the fundamentals of democracy. They could be taught stories of the founding fathers and taken to field trips of historical places. Youth empowerment is vital, and if these children are given responsibilities in classrooms at a very early age, then they learn civic engagement automatically. Give children a project to work on, and they will know how to do it together.

It would be even better to create conversations around community service and civic engagement and see what children know and enlighten them on the concept of helping each other for the common good. The way it works is to start conversations every day in schools and have children exchange ideas. This will help build their understanding of civic engagement. If we want to equip our children with the tools to participate in civic engagement, we need to create that understanding first, and it needs to then move to the home where parents continue the same conversations and talk

16   *Youth civic engagement activities are critical for empowering young people and bettering society. (2016, March 3). Children International.   https://www.children.org/learn-more/newsroom/2015/aug/youth-civic-engagement-activities*

about how things were in their times. The more knowledge our children have, the more they will be encouraged to participate in civic engagement activities. Our youth are our lifelines, so we must educate and preserve them.

Of, By, and For the Students

> *"Being the Queen is not all about singing, and being a diva is not all about singing. It has much to do with your service to people. And your social contributions to your community and your civic contributions as well."*

– Aretha Franklin

One thing I saw in my college years was the presence of a student government, and that fascinated me a lot. It was incredible how students elected representatives among themselves to communicate student issues with the administration. They would run several clubs and plan activities as part of student government. A president would be elected in the same way as our democratic process works in selecting one for the country. These are incredible opportunities for students to participate in civic engagement but at a collegiate level and gain an understanding of responsibilities and duties. I must recommend every college student to take part in this as the learning opportunities are excellent. From marketing to budgeting to planning and negotiating with administration, you get to be part of every process and make a change for students at the institution. It's a superb opportunity and a great way to learn civic engagement in a hands-on environment. If you're ever interested in politics in the future, then getting your hands wet in student government is the way to go.

United Nations

> *"All human beings are born free and equal in dignity and rights. They are endowed with reason and conscience and should act towards one another in a spirit of brotherhood."*

- Article 1 Universal Declaration of Human Rights, United Nations

The United Nations holds an International Youth Day that encourages children worldwide to participate in civic engagement activities, and some are even organized by them solely. For example, in 2015, there were a few initiatives on IYD 2015. One of those programs was the International Youth Community Reporters Program. The official website states the following about this exciting activity:

> *"Children International's Community Youth Reporters program empowers youth by giving them a voice while helping them develop journalism skills. The youth learn about news writing, interviewing, photography and videography, making them a group that's well-suited to capture the importance of civic engagement activities around them and communicate that information*

> *to others. For the IYD campaign, they are sharing*
> *photos of their peers participating in Children*
> *International civic engagement activities, including*
> *photos of youth learning about social and financial*
> *education, participating in sports programs,*
> *and receiving leadership training. Each photo*
> *is accompanied by a caption that explains the*
> *significance of the activity."*[17]

Such activities offer tremendous benefits. According to the website, "These activities are important because they teach life and leadership skills, which empower youth, help them become self-reliant adults, and encourage them to contribute to society. Social and financial education, for example, teaches young people their rights, responsibilities and how to save, plan and budget their resources. Involving youth in organized sports programs teaches them teamwork, conflict resolution, and perseverance."[18]

This fantastic opportunity conducted by the United Nations is an excellent example of how schools and communities can empower the youth to take action and become community

17   *Youth civic engagement activities are critical for empowering young people and bettering society. (2016, March 3). Children International.   https://www.children.org/learn-more/newsroom/2015/aug/youth-civic-engagement-activities*

18   *Youth civic engagement activities are critical for empowering young people and bettering society. (2016, March 3). Children International.   https://www.children.org/learn-more/newsroom/2015/aug/youth-civic-engagement-activities*

warriors. We have to realize that these children are our future, and we need to ensure that they grow with civic responsibility and become effective and influential leaders as adults in whatever field they choose to be in. If possible, it's excellent to have a civics class in every grade the children study in their school years. Community service must be made compulsory at every grade level so our children can go out in the field and help with community welfare. They could visit nursing homes and volunteer or feed the homeless. Obviously, bake sales and similar activities to raise funding to battle poverty are all excellent initiatives.

We discussed the Model United Nations Program in the previous chapter, and that's squarely aimed at young adults. Several of the student delegates are either pursuing political science and international relations as their majors. You'd also find many history, business, and economics majors because these are all fields that could lead these young adults into global politics and foreign service. Almost every college in the US has a Model United Nations club where members would join and participate in mock debates and dialogue sessions and research different countries and their foreign policy. Other activities would include discussing global events and current affairs and how different countries view these events. Students should be highly encouraged to participate in Model UN activities as these are fun learning opportunities to emulate world leaders and discuss foreign policy. Our students need to know what the rest of the world thinks of us and what we think of them. Every country has different forms of governance, and these students can increase their awareness of global politics by knowing these.

Democracy

"All human beings are born free and equal in dignity and rights. They are endowed with reason and conscience and should act towards one another in a spirit of brotherhood."

- Article 1 Universal Declaration of Human Rights, United Nations

I would highly recommend children from at least the middle school level to learn how American politics work and the different branches of government. One would learn these in American history, but a dedicated class on these would be an excellent way to teach children about the two major parties and how the voting process works on a state and federal level. They could learn about the judiciary, Congress - including its two different houses, and the presidency. They could be taught how the Electoral College process works. Roleplaying activities would include a mock Congress with a senate and house of representatives. Children could play the roles of senators and even run for mock presidential elections with proper campaigns. This would give them a very realistic perspective of how politics work in the form of fun activities wherein all students would be able to participate. Class teachers can encourage their students to send letters to local and state representatives airing concerns that matter to them and their communities. These are wonderful opportunities for our children to engage with their local leaders and let them know that their voice matters and should be heard and acted upon. Getting a response back from these representatives would encourage the children further to communicate with them.

At the same time, students should be encouraged to join the student council and get elected in different positions. Leadership positions at an early age give these children the chance to build leadership and teamwork skills. The same goes for chairing various school clubs and committees where they could have hands-on opportunities to exercise leadership and work with their peers to improve things in school and address students' concerns.

See, if we're part of a country that works on the principle and notion of a government for the people, by the people, and of the people, these children should know that they're part of these people too. Their voice counts, and they need to learn these principles at an early age, so they know what it means to live in a free country. We're the champions of democracy, and this needs to be instilled in our children so they can take up the responsibility in the future for continuing the progress our nation has made since independence.

At the end of the day, civic engagement is about working together to make a difference in people's lives and serving the community. It's about learning skills, knowledge, and values that allow us to be effective community leaders and representatives. It's about promoting community welfare and initiating programs to make it happen. It's both political and non-political because we can only bring about the change in the communities we serve and live in via both means. Whether you're an activist, teacher, politician, community leader, law-enforcement official, health practitioner, or environmentalist, we all have to work together to bring about the greater good for the greater amount of people. We need to give back to the communities because it has given us so much, from housing to education and more.

It is our duty to help our children understand these concepts so they can apply them as adults and school programs are some of the best ways to do so. We have touched upon different methods and strategies to involve our children in civic engagement activities via educational programs. Still, there are most definitely more ways than what is discussed in this chapter. We can always think outside the box to get our children involved because civic engagement is our duty and responsibility. We need to raise our children right and educate them with these principles so they know what it means to live in a democratic country and improve our communities. We must make a pact to ensure our children are taught these values in schools, and our schools must make it a huge focus as well. It is only then; we can safeguard the future of our country, and we most definitely can.

I want to end this chapter with a quote from the youngest Nobel Peace Prize winner, and this young girl from Pakistan made history by surviving a bullet shot to the head and fighting for education and women's rights. She is undoubtedly an excellent individual, and I am absolutely honored and humbled to include her quote as it speaks volumes. She is a role model for not just the youth but for all aspiring and current leaders of the world. Her life is of fighting for education for all, and she is one shining star that will continue to shine bright, and her light will lead the way forward for all of us. She is one of our many beacons of hope, and it is people like her that reinforce my trust in humanity and our everlasting and unwavering spirit. She is none other Malala Yousufzai and this one quote of hers shows why civic engagement is so crucial for the youth of the world.

"Let us remember: One book, one pen, one child, and one teacher can change the world."

- Malala Yousafzai

Chapter 9:

Community and Civic Engagement in times of the Coronavirus

"Everyone must leave something behind when he dies...something your hand touched some way, so your soul has somewhere to go when you die. It doesn't matter what you do, so long as you change something from the way it was before you touched it into something that's like you after you take your hands away."

- Ray Bradbury, Fahrenheit 451

We live in turbulent times, and even though there has been some stability regarding the coronavirus, new strains have developed. The coronavirus pandemic is still far from over globally, which has had severe ramifications in our communities. While this has been touched upon in previous chapters, we will be examining ways to handle SOPs, regulations, and community issues during the pandemic. There are several ways to engage with our community leaders in resolving issues that have plagued our communities due to the pandemic. We will be revisiting ideas that have been discussed in previous chapters and bringing in new ways to tackle everyday problems and how our community leaders can make our lives easier. It is highly imperative to examine current such engagements and how we can build similar models in our communities and improve them.

The coronavirus disease and pandemic changed our lives and has taken countless lives. There has been a series of information and misinformation. This is a time where we all need to come together to educate the masses on the truth and weed out misinformation, lies, and conspiracy theories that are only misguiding than educating. Civic education is the need of the hour. We need to take ownership and leadership and help eradicate misinformation so people take the right actions and stay safe. The world we live in has an abundance of information, thanks to the internet. Social media and instant messaging apps, such as WhatsApp, are full of information that could be either true, false, or just plain conspiracy theories. So, who can we trust to save our lives? The conspiracy theorists call themselves whistleblowers, while mainstream media and social media platforms are working together to eliminate misinformation.

Similarly, global and national health bodies, such as the CDC (Centers for Disease Control and Prevention) and WHO (World Health Organization), are tackling misinformation 24/7/365. The world is starving for the truth, and there are so many supposed truths going around, but we don't know who to believe. As the X-Files show once said, "The truth is out there;" it most certainly is. We are the ones responsible for finding it and spreading it. If we don't, we could end up causing chaos and disorder, and we won't have anyone to blame but ourselves to cause this mess. Knowledge is power, and we must use it very wisely. Therefore, we must curb misinformation and spread the truth as much as possible because great power comes with great responsibility. At the same time, we must never forget that with great responsibility comes great power as well.

Waking up the World

"All human beings are born free and equal in dignity and rights. They are endowed with reason and conscience and should act towards one another in a spirit of brotherhood."

- Article 1 Universal Declaration of Human Rights, United Nations

Every day, we wake up to check our social media accounts and our instant messaging apps; we see someone sharing propaganda against the vaccines and claiming that the information is from whistleblowers being censored by mainstream media to protect their interests. This causes confusion, and some get caught in the hype to disbelieve information that is true. Fact-checkers are constantly working to disprove conspiracy theories, and several have been proven false. That doesn't end as something new shows up. That causes fear, and fear causes anxiety, which has a much worse impact than the coronavirus disease itself.

All this misinformation helps no one and prevents doctors from doing their jobs and administering vaccines that can help prevent the spread of the virus and decrease its symptoms. You'll see labels pop underneath every post that's related to the vaccines, just like you'll see them on cigarette boxes. The warning signs are there to let us know that the news presented to us on social media platforms is from unverified sources or completely misconstrued. These are hoaxes or just someone trying to discredit the vaccines. There is a lot of hard work and effort gone on into the vaccines, but there is an alternative worldview that "Big Pharma" is profiteering from the vaccines, and this is all a setup. Bill Gates and other "elites" are involved in depopulation efforts, and the vaccines inject you with nanoparticles that apparently connect with 5G towers to control us. All of this sounds very far-fetched, but there is a sizeable population of the world that does subscribe to this alternate reality. The point is we've become a very gullible nation and can believe in anything that is presented to us from a somewhat credible source because there is this alternative thinking process that the mainstream media is spreading the fear of the pandemic, and it doesn't exist.

This sets dangerous precedence where the health bodies use mainstream media and influencers to spread the truth while that same truth is considered propaganda from alternative thinkers. Obviously, this alternative thought process is expected to get people thinking that we're all being made fools, but unfortunately, the reality is far from this far-fetched science fiction nonsense. If you or your family member has suffered from the COVID-19 virus, you know it's not easy to stay in quarantine and face its effects.

We all know that COVID-19 can take the life out of you, but there is good news: Health experts say that vaccines reduce the symptoms, so your COVID-19 quarantine time is not as difficult as it would be otherwise, and that has been seen in several real-life cases too. That being said, there have been cases of side effects from moderate to severe. Therefore, health experts have always advised consulting doctors before being vaccinated and getting a health checkup to ensure there are no underlying conditions that vaccines could aggravate. All of these warnings and side effects are clearly mentioned on WHO and CDC websites. That's the official source of information to go to. If you don't live in the US, you should also consult your local health bodies instead of unverifiable or uncreditable sources that are made viral on the internet.

Brave New World

"The world as we have created it is a process of our thinking. It cannot be changed without changing our thinking."

- Albert Einstein

We live in a brave new world today. Thanks to COVID-19, we have become a lot braver and stronger than before. We have faced so much together, and perhaps, for the first time in so many decades, the world came together as one to tackle an ongoing pandemic. The pandemic impacted everyone's lives, forcing most people across the globe to stay at home and work from there. There were layoffs, downsizing, and furloughs, as companies worldwide and locally were facing problems. Lives had dramatically changed as retail stores were now forced to stay shut, and you could only order simple things like groceries online. Communities gathered together to support those laid off and furloughed. The government was under pressure as they had to take care of several unemployed workers via unemployment benefits. We had now transitioned into what became popularly known as "the new normal."

The new normal was a time when civic engagement was rampant, especially on social media. Social media became an outlet for everyone across the globe to voice their concerns and frustrations regarding the pandemic. Whether people were on Facebook, YouTube, or Twitter, they went live talking about how the pandemic changed everyone's lives. The television channels also used these social media tools such as Google Meet and Zoom to reach out to correspondents for news broadcasts. Social media kept buzzing with people experiencing transitions in their lives by being at home most times working, finding work, or freelancing.

We saw tremendous change in how people became very entrepreneurial in terms of making ends meet. New entrepreneurs took birth on Facebook and Instagram and got their followers to market their goods. The pandemic was a time where citizens decided to take matters into their hands. Whether it was to start a business or raise awareness on social issues, people embraced the new normal and access to social media to project their thoughts and become keyboard warriors. This was a time of much-needed change, and citizens were taking charge.

Perhaps, the biggest turning point for citizens was how there were no live events because people were confined to homes. All public gatherings were off-limits, so the only way to voice concerns was online. Therefore, we saw a revolution taking place, and social media platforms were at the forefront of it. Even more interesting was the challenge of holding elections in the middle of the pandemic. That perhaps became one of the biggest talking points of civic engagement in the pandemic.

Democracy! (Alternate Title: Chinese Democracy)

"Power concedes nothing without a demand. It never did, and it never will. Find out just what any people will quietly submit to, and you have found out the exact measure of injustice and wrong which will be imposed upon them, and these will continue till they are resisted with either words or blows or with both. The limits of tyrants are prescribed by the endurance of those whom they oppress."

- Fredrick Douglas

This is the first time in the 21st century when American citizens elected a president during a pandemic. It was Trump vs. Biden, and what a contest it was. I don't think there could be any bigger example of civic engagement in the pandemic than what we witnessed most of 2020. Imagine how both candidates competed without televised debates in front of people and reached out to voters the traditional way via electoral campaigns. These were mostly done online, but there was an election, and a new president was sworn into office regardless of how things changed. When we talk about debates, they were done online and not face to face with the public as they would be. Still, they served the purpose as the US is fairly progressive when it comes to online civic engagement and most of the population has access to at least one internet-enabled device.

The debates were televised in studios or via collegiate campuses, but no live audience was present and just the candidates, crew, and a moderator. As the debates went on, the keyboard warriors were ready to voice their opinions online during the debates as well as before and after it. The pandemic didn't allow democracy to falter, and the will of the people did prevail. Our nation was founded on the principles of democracy, and the system had to evolve, but the process was still the same. People did vote, and there were SOPs involved to ensure that social distancing was practiced.

The idea here is that civic engagement will stay regardless of the pandemic. As usual, there was in-person voting, absentee, and mail-in voting.

According to Pew Research, "A slim majority of voters (54%) say they voted in person this November, compared with 46% who voted by absentee or mail-in ballot. About one-quarter (27%)

report having voted in person on Election Day, and
an identical share say they voted in person before
Election Day."[19]

As you can see clearly, democracy wasn't impacted much at all, and people did come out to vote regardless of the pandemic. I would say that voting is one of the main civic duties of any citizen, so no one would forego their right and responsibility to vote, and we saw a new president take charge. Although it wasn't completely peaceful, a transition of power did take place, but that is another story. The January 6 insurrection could be a form of negative civic engagement and bordering very much close to anarchy whether you oppose Donald Trump or side him. Any form of civic protest that turns violent or encourages vandalism should never be condoned whatsoever. I would hope that our citizens use nonviolent means of protest because violence doesn't help anyone. It is never the solution to any problem. If Trump supporters have an issue with the Biden administration, they can voice their concerns in the right ways and hold them accountable via their votes when the next election happens in 2024.

19   3. *The voting experience in 2020.* (2020, November 20). *Pew Research Center - US Politics & Policy. https://www.pewresearch.org/ politics/2020/11/20/the-voting-experience-in-2020/*

World in Motion

*"No matter what people tell you, words and ideas
can change the world."*

- NH. Kleinbaum, Dead Poets Society

Whether there's a pandemic or not, the world keeps on spinning. Thanks to the progress in technology and science, social media has allowed people to stay in touch and do things they may otherwise not do. Social media has allowed us to be more aware of the world around us, and there is more transparency than ever was previously. Everyone now has a voice, and when so many voices sing the same song, the world does take notice. The world has become such a small place that problems are daily being solved because we have easy access to our community leaders. We had discussed connecting with the community and civic leaders via social media and perhaps holding town halls through Zoom or Google Meet. Thanks to vaccinations, life is returning slowly and steadily to the way we were, but we're not quite there yet. There's a lot to do to tackle misinformation and define SOPs, which can be done via outreach to our community and civic leaders.

The world will never stop moving no matter what happens because humans will evolve and find new ways to tackle problems. We will always have a voice, and our civic leaders will hear us out. The pandemic has seen so many voices being raised, and that's essentially a very good thing.

Hopefully, we can completely unite together as one and deal with this pandemic for good and others as and when they come.

> *"What you do makes a difference, and you have to decide what kind of difference you want to make."*

> **- Jane Goodall**

Chapter 10:
Final Words and a Look to the Future

"The world as we have created it is a process of our thinking. It cannot be changed without changing our thinking."

- Albert Einstein

We all have a responsibility to attain knowledge because knowledge is power and with great power comes great responsibility. With great responsibility comes great power too. I can't stress enough how important all three of these components are when it comes to civic engagement because leadership and community both come with responsibility. We need to be responsible for ourselves and our fellow brothers and sisters. I want to use this opportunity to leave you all with some words of wisdom that should hopefully resonate with you long after you close the book for the final time. When there are no more pages to turn, we will need to absorb and process this food for thought. I would like to leave things on a powerful and positive note. These discussions should continue beyond the scope of this book and be an ongoing exercise.

The future of civic and community engagement depends on how we act and behave with others as community members and leaders. We must be more active from the present day so we can create future leaders and responsible citizens of the future.

We've come to the final chapter, and after nine chapters discussing different facets of civic engagement and its history, there is perhaps more to explore on this theme. The idea behind writing this book is not to cover everything on civic engagement per se, but it is to educate and create awareness of its importance and why it matters so much today as it has mattered to people for over several decades and more. Civic engagement has been the fabric of our society for centuries now. Democracy has allowed civic engagement to occur, and that's how our societies have been shaped now. We've come a long way from where we were in our early days. We've seen civil war, civil rights movement, global issues, current affairs, world wars, political conflicts, military campaigns, epidemics, pandemics, and even tragedies such as Pearl Harbor and 9/11. These have given rise to so much civic engagement, and social media has now taken it to a much higher level. There are no barriers between leaders and followers and, I would dare say, voters. We've learned valuable lessons from our history, and in the future, we need to keep civic engagement at the forefront.

I want to take this opportunity to reflect on the takeaways of each chapter because the idea has always been to inform and educate. I know that a single book isn't enough to convey everything but at least enough for us to gain an understanding of civic engagement. Civic engagement is something we do daily, almost unknowingly, because we're so hooked to the news and comment on it daily through social media.

I mentioned the term keyboard warriors in the previous chapter because it's true. Several community issues get discussed on these platforms, and sometimes several people get together to raise awareness and become a combined voice for those causes. As I have said before, every individual has a voice, which has to be heard. Therefore, these voices become a larger voice on these social media platforms and eventually make a difference. The civic leaders are present on these platforms to address those issues, which was unprecedented in decades that came before.

Back to the Future

We started off the book by discussing civic engagement and its purpose. We gave it a definition and examined its importance in the world today and throughout history. We discussed every citizen's civic duty and went on towards understanding how civic engagement is part and parcel of democracy. It's clear we've come a long way since we became a free nation, and a lot of that has to do with civic engagement. The idea of giving a voice to people is as important as it is to civic leaders as the latter gets chosen from the former. Thanks to social media, there is no filter or barrier between them and us, and that's a great thing. At the same time, accountability is important on both sides. Power and responsibility go hand in hand, and that's where accountability comes in. Leaders make several campaigns and promises but should be held accountable for their promises because they were elected for the same reasons at the end of the day. At the same time, knowledge is power, and the more knowledge you have, you can select the right leader among yourselves. That's the true essence of giving power to the people.

We have to stick to the very principles our nation was founded on: of the people, by the people, and for the people. That's how democracy works and should never change. Our democratic leaders haven't been perfect and have committed blunders but also have done well too. We even profiled several presidents of the recent past and examined their successes and failures from a very neutral perspective. As we all know, one person's freedom fighter is another one's terrorist. Perspectives should be looked at neutrally respecting both views but also figuring out via education and awareness which one is more likely true of the other. Our schools and universities have been budding platforms for teaching children civic engagement via student-run clubs and societies, student councils, student government, and community services.

Young adults and children all benefit from these activities as it helps build a greater understanding. Model United Nations conferences allow young adults from high schools and colleges to participate in student-run simulations of United Nations conferences as every school represents delegates of different countries. It increases awareness of different nations and their cultures plus global perspectives. It's an amazing learning experience, and every student should take advantage of it, even if it is for fun. If you're lucky, you get to be a delegate and speak on the floor of the actual UN General Assembly in New York City.

Things have changed drastically in the last 12 to 15 months, thanks to the COVID-19 pandemic. This hasn't been the best time for us as we had been forced to work from home and be confined there for the better part of the year. Social distancing became the norm but gave rise to keyboard warriors participating in civic engagement on social media platforms. The economic impact is known widely, but thanks to vaccines, the new normal is wearing off slowly but steadily. We now have to combat misinformation as it creates fear and misguides people causing more stress and resulting in serious physical illnesses just because we believed something shared on the internet that came from unverifiable and uncredited sources. Finally, we even elected a new president in the pandemic despite several issues.

Tomorrow Never Dies

"Yesterday I was clever, so I wanted to change the world. Today I am wise, so I am changing myself."

- Rumi

There's a lot to write, but I would perhaps leave it for another book. At this point, I want to look toward the future and tell you all that it does look bright because we're survivors.

The human race, having survived the pandemic, is ready for anything. Although the pandemic is still the pandemic, it's being contained despite new strains. I don't see the need to fear the future because we have the gift of civic engagement and can use it to highlight important issues, whether racial, religious, cultural, or anything of importance to us. We need to use our platforms for positive and impactful endeavors and help our fellow citizens as leaders and community members because they deserve the best from us. We deserve the best from ourselves, too. one person can make a difference, and more than that could change the world forever.

I hope to wake up to a better tomorrow because civic engagement is key to a bright and prosperous future where the truth shall prevail and leaders serve their people justly and responsibly. We need to educate ourselves and elect the right people in power because together, we can change the world by simply acting responsibly! Please read below the quote from one of Hollywood's highly acclaimed actors because such words speak volumes and are my parting gift to you all. Thank you all so very much for being part of this journey with me. I hope to see you on the flip side very soon.

I would highly appreciate it if you could spread the message of civic engagement far and wide to your friends, families, and loved ones so they can keep the spirit of civic engagement alive for generations on. Be responsible for yourself and others, and that's how all of us can change the world, one person at a time!

"The way to change the world is through individual responsibility and taking local action in your own community."

- Jeff Bridges

About the Author

Ronnie L. Smith is a citizen, small business owner
and government servant who has served on several
committees across various sectors including non-profits and
governments at the local level as well as regional levels; he
also attends schools to achieve his education goals.